SELECTED ESSAYS
ON THE DYNAMICS OF
THE CAPITALIST ECONOMY
1933–1970

SELECTED ESSAYS ON THE DYNAMICS OF THE CAPITALIST ECONOMY
1933–1970

MICHAŁ KALECKI

CAMBRIDGE
AT THE UNIVERSITY PRESS
1971

Published by the Syndics of the Cambridge University Press
Bentley House, 200 Euston Road, London NW1 2DB
American Branch: 32 East 57th Street, New York, N.Y.10022

This selection and Introduction © Cambridge University Press 1971

Library of Congress Catalogue Card Number: 78–123667

ISBN: 0 521 07983 7

Printed in Great Britain
at the University Printing House, Cambridge
(Brooke Crutchley, University Printer)

CONTENTS

*Full details on original sources and dates of publication of each
chapter are given in the author's Introduction, p. vii*

PUBLISHER'S NOTE

Michał Kalecki died on 17 April 1970, before this book went to the printer. We are very grateful for the help of Dr D. M. Nuti, who has seen the book through the press.

INTRODUCTION

This volume of my selected essays includes what I consider my main contributions to the theory of dynamics of the capitalist economy, published over the thirty-seven years 1933–70. In each case the year of publication of the version in question is given and if there was a different earlier version this date is also added. The book is subdivided into three parts.

The first part includes three papers published in 1933, 1934 and 1935 in Polish before Keynes' *General Theory* appeared, and containing, I believe, its essentials (an English translation was first published in *Studies in the Theory of Business Cycles, 1933–1939*, Basil Blackwell, Oxford, 1967). In addition in this part the reader will find a short paper on commodity, income and capital taxation published in the *Economic Journal*, 1937.

The second part consists of chapters excerpted from my *Theory of Economic Dynamics*, George Allen and Unwin, London, 1954. But in all instances these are final versions of earlier papers or chapters of earlier books. 'Costs and Prices', 'Determinants of Investment' and 'The Business Cycle' appeared in their first versions in *Studies in Economic Dynamics*, George Allen and Unwin, 1943. The basic idea of 'Distribution of National Income' was presented (in a rather imperfect form) in *Econometrica*, 1938. An earlier version of 'The Determinants of Profits' appeared in the *Economic Journal* 1942, and the first version of 'Determination of Income and Consumption' can be found in *Essays in Economic Fluctuations*, George Allen and Unwin, 1939. 'Entrepreneurial Capital and Investment' is a new version of 'Principle of Increasing Risk' published in *Economica*, 1937.

In the third part are included: 'Political Aspects of Full Employment', published first in the *Political Quarterly*, 1943; 'The Problem of Effective Demand with Tugan-Baranovski and

Introduction

Rosa Luxemburg' published (in Polish) in *Ekonomista*, 1967; 'The Class Struggle and the Distribution of National Income', published in *Kyklos*, 1971 and finally 'Trend and the Business Cycle', published in the *Economic Journal*, 1968.

It is interesting to notice that the theory of effective demand, already clearly formulated in the first papers, remains unchanged in all the relevant writings, as do my views on the distribution of national income. However, there is a continuous search for new solutions in the theory of investment decisions, where even the last paper represents—for better or for worse—a novel approach.

The essays brought together in this volume have in some cases been abbreviated, or slightly (chiefly stylistically) adjusted, but in no case substantially supplemented.

M. KALECKI

Warsaw

PART I

1. OUTLINE OF A THEORY
OF THE BUSINESS CYCLE

[1933]

ASSUMPTIONS

We shall consider a *closed* economic system, *devoid of trends*, i.e.
one which returns to its original state after each cycle. In
addition we shall make the following assumptions.

1. *Gross real profits.* By gross real profits P we understand the
aggregate real income of capitalists including depreciation per
unit of time consisting of their consumption and saving

$$P = C + A \qquad (1.1)$$

Thus C denotes all goods which are consumed by capitalists
and A includes—since we abstract from workers' savings or their
'capitalist' incomes—all goods which are used in the reproduction and expansion of fixed capital as well as the increase in
inventories. In the future A will be referred to as gross accumulation.†

The personal consumption of capitalists is relatively inelastic.
Let us assume that C consists of a constant part B_0 and a part
which is proportionate to gross profits:

$$C = B_0 + \lambda P \qquad (1.2)$$

where λ is a small constant.

---

† The national income is equal on the one hand to the sum of profits and wages,
and on the other, to the sum of: (1) the reproduction and expansion of fixed
capital and the increase in inventories A; (2) the consumption of capitalists; and
(3) the consumption of workers. Since the latter is equal to wages, profits are equal
to $C + A$.

From equations (1) and (2) we obtain:

$$P = B_0 + \lambda P + A$$

$$P = \frac{B_0 + A}{1 - \lambda} \tag{1.3}$$

i.e. the gross real profits P are proportionate to the sum $B_0 + A$ of the constant part of capitalists' consumption B_0 and the gross accumulation A.

The gross accumulation A is according to the above equal to the sum of the production of investment goods and the increase in inventories.† *For the sake of simplicity we assume that aggregate inventories remain constant throughout the trade cycle.*

It follows from the above assumptions that the real profits P are proportionate to $B_0 + A$, where B_0 denotes the constant part of the capitalists' consumption, and A the gross accumulation which is equal to the production of investment goods.

2. *Investment.* We assume that the period of construction ϑ is the same for any investment project. This of course is not in fact the case. ϑ should be considered as the average construction period, and our assumption that the construction period is the same for all types of investment must be considered as one of the simplifications introduced in our model.

Three stages should be distinguished in the investment activity: (1) investment orders, i.e. all types of orders for investment goods for the sake of reproduction and expansion of the capital equipment, the volume of which per unit of time will be denoted by I; (2) production of investment goods A which, according to the above, is equal to the gross accumulation; (3) deliveries of finished equipment per unit of time D‡

† We do not include capital under construction in inventories; a change in the volume of such capital is covered by 'production of investment goods'; however, this item does not cover changes in inventories of other investment goods (e.g. in inventories of steel or cement). Changes in this type of inventory must be thus included in 'the increase in inventories'.

‡ A and D differ in that A is the production of investment goods in general, and D is the production of finished investment goods. It follows that the difference $A - D$ is equal to the increment of capital under construction per unit of time.

The relation between I and D is simple: deliveries D at the time t are equal to the investment orders I placed at the time $t-\vartheta$; thus the curve D is the curve I shifted by the time-lag ϑ (see Fig. 1.1).

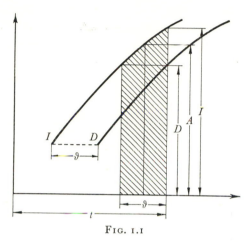

FIG. 1.1

The relation between the production of investment goods A and investment orders I is somewhat more complicated. The shaded area of the trapezium (Fig. 1.1) is equal to the value of orders placed during a period of the length ϑ ending at the time t, and thus equal to the portfolio of orders at the time t which we shall denote by W. Indeed, since the completing of each order takes the time ϑ all orders which come within the shaded area have not yet been completed, while all equipment previously ordered has already been installed. Next, production of investment goods is equal to the portfolio of orders W divided by the period of construction:

$$A = \frac{W}{\vartheta} \qquad (1.4)$$

Indeed, if each order is to be completed during the time ϑ then $1/\vartheta$ of its volume must be completed per unit of time; thus to the portfolio of orders W, there corresponds the production of investment goods W/ϑ.

3

It follows that A is equal to the shaded area of the trapezium divided by ϑ. If the upper side of the trapezium were rectilinear, the production of investment goods A would, at the time t, be equal to the median of the trapezium and thus to the investment orders at the time $t - \frac{1}{2}\vartheta$. If the upper side of the trapezium is curvilinear, this will be only approximately true. *The production of investment goods at the time t is thus approximately equal to the investment orders at the time $t - \frac{1}{2}\vartheta$.* Thus the curve A is approximately identical with the curve I shifted by $\frac{1}{2}\vartheta$ (see Fig. 1.2).

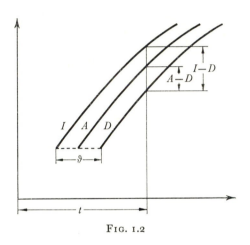

FIG. 1.2

It should be noticed that the difference $I - D$ is equal to the increase of the portfolio of orders per unit of time, while the difference $A - D$ is equal to the increase of capital under construction per unit of time. (This was already pointed out in the footnote ‡ to page 2.)

3. *Changes in the volume of capital equipment.* Let the volume of capital equipment at a given time be denoted by K. Its change during a given period is equal to the difference between deliveries of new equipment and the volume of productive assets going out of use. Denoting the change of the capital equipment K per unit of time by $\Delta K/\Delta t$, deliveries of new equipment per unit

4

of time—as above—by D, and the replacement requirements due to particular productive assets' going out of use per unit of time by U, we obtain:

$$\frac{\Delta K}{\Delta t} = D - U \qquad (1.5)$$

We may assume that replacement requirements remain at a constant level in the course of the business cycle. It is true that the volume of capital equipment K shows in fact small fluctuations, and it might seem therefore that in the part I of the cycle (see Fig. 1.3),

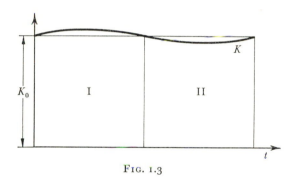

FIG. 1.3

when K is greater than the average, the required replacements are higher than the average as well. However, it should be noticed that in part I the increase in the capital equipment consists of 'young' assets of low 'mortality', because the 'life' of these assets is known to be considerably longer than the length of one cycle (15–30 years as compared with 8–12). Thus fluctuations of the replacement requirements can be considered negligible.

The constant level of replacement requirements U is equal to the average D_0 of deliveries of new equipment D over one cycle, because we assumed that our system is devoid of trends and the volume of capital equipment returns at the end of the cycle to its original size. Furthermore, for the same reason the average over one cycle of investment orders I_0, of production of invest-

5

ment goods A_0 and of deliveries of new equipment D_0 are all equal. We thus obtain:

$$U = I_0 = A_0 = D_0 \qquad (1.6)$$

4. *Investment orders as a function of gross profitability and of the rate of interest.* The volume of investment orders D at a given time depends on the anticipated net profitability. Thus if entrepreneurs consider investing a capital k in the construction of capital equipment, they will estimate in the first place the anticipated gross profit p. From this we must deduct: (1) the depreciation βk (β being the depreciation rate); (2) the interest on capital k amounting to ik (i being the rate of interest); (3) the interest on the future circulating capital which, if its relation to fixed capital k is denoted by γ, amounts to $i\gamma k$. The anticipated profitability of investment in fixed capital k will thus be

$$\frac{p - \beta k - ik - i\gamma k}{k} = \frac{p}{k} - \beta - i(1 + \gamma)$$

The coefficients β and γ may be considered to remain constant throughout the trade cycle; i is the rate of interest at a given time. The anticipated gross profitability P/K may be estimated from the actual gross profitability of existing plant. We have already denoted the volume of capital equipment at a given time by K and the aggregate gross profit by P; consequently the gross profitability of existing plant is P/K. Thus we may conclude that p/k is estimated on the basis of P/K, and that the investment orders at a given time depend on the gross profitability P/K and on the rate of interest i.

It should be added that this is not the investment orders I that should be considered a function of P/K and i, but rather the ratio of I to the volume of capital equipment K, i.e. I/K; indeed, if P and K increase in the same proportion, P/K will remain unchanged, while I is likely to increase in the same proportion as P and K. Thus we arrive finally at the relation:

$$\frac{I}{K} = f\left(\frac{P}{K}, i\right) \qquad (1.7)$$

6

where f is an increasing function of P/K and a diminishing function of i.

It is known that in the course of the trade cycle the rate of interest rises in the upswing and falls in the downswing. When we come to develop our theory, we shall try to explain this connection (see pp. 13–14). At the moment we shall accept it *a priori*, and on this basis we shall make the following simplifying assumption. *The rate of interest i is an increasing function of the gross profitability P/K.*

From this assumption and the equation (1.7) it follows that I/K is a function of P/K:

$$\frac{I}{K} = F\left(\frac{P}{K}\right) \tag{1.8}$$

Let us also assume that *the rate of interest increases sufficiently slowly in relation to the gross profitability P/K for F to be an increasing function.*

Since, as was shown above, the gross profit P is proportionate to $B_0 + A$ where B is the constant part of capitalists' consumption and the gross accumulation A is equal to the production of investment goods, P/K is proportionate to $(B_0 + A)/K$ and the equation (1.8) may be written as follows:

$$\frac{I}{K} = \varphi\left(\frac{B_0 + A}{K}\right) \tag{1.9}$$

where φ is an increasing function.

Moreover, we assume that φ is a linear function i.e.

$$\frac{I}{K} = m\frac{B_0 + A}{K} - n \tag{1.10}$$

The constant m must be positive since φ is an increasing function. Equation (1.10) may be written in the form:

$$I = m(B_0 + A) - nK \tag{1.10a}$$

We shall now show that n must be positive. From the equation (1.10a) it follows that

$$n = \frac{m(B_0 + A) - I}{K}$$

7

I representing the orders for goods used for the reproduction and expansion of capital equipment remains always positive; it may, however, possibly approach the zero level. Let us imagine that *I* falls below the positive value mB_0. For values of *I* less than mB_0 the expression $[m(B_0 + A) - I]/K$ is greater than mA/K, i.e. mA/K will then be less than *n*. Since, however, the coefficient *m* is positive, as shown above, and since *A* (production of investment goods) and *K* (volume of capital equipment) are also positive, it follows that the coefficient *n* must be positive.

According to equation (1.10a), *in which the coefficient m and n are positive, the volume of investment orders I is an increasing function of the gross accumulation A and a diminishing function of the volume of capital equipment K.*

THE MECHANISM OF THE TRADE CYCLE

1. The main conclusions of the argument in the preceding chapter may be stated as follows:

(*a*) The time-lag between the placing of investment orders and deliveries of new equipment is ϑ; the curve of deliveries *D* is shifted from the curve of investment orders *I* by the time ϑ. The curve of the production of investment goods *A* is shifted from the curve of investment orders approximately by $\frac{1}{2}\vartheta$.

(*b*) In our system the production of investment goods *A* is equal to the gross accumulation (since inventories remain at a constant level).

(*c*) Deliveries of new fixed assets *D* lead to an increase in the volume of the capital equipment by $D - U$, where *U* denotes the replacement requirements. *U* remains constant throughout the trade cycle and its value is equal to the average D_0 of deliveries *D* over a full cycle. D_0 is also equal to the average of investment orders I_0 and the average production of investment goods A_0.

(*d*) Investment orders *I* are an increasing function of the gross accumulation *A* and a decreasing function of the volume of capital equipment:

$$I = m(B_0 + A) - nK$$

where m and n are positive coefficients, and B_0 is the constant part of capitalists' consumption.

2. These points already enable us to say something about the mechanism of the trade cycle. An increase in investment orders calls forth an increase in the production of investment goods which is equal to the gross accumulation. This in turn causes a further increase in investment activity, as indicated by equation (1.10a). However, after an interval of time ϑ has elapsed from the time when investment orders have exceeded the level of replacement requirements, the volume of capital equipment starts to increase. Initially this restrains the rate at which investment activity is increasing, and at a later stage causes a decline in investment orders.

In particular it is impossible to stabilize investment activity at a level exceeding the replacement requirements. Indeed, if investment orders remain at a constant level the production of investment goods, which is equal to the gross accumulation, will remain unchanged as well, while capital equipment expands, investment being greater than replacement requirements. Under such conditions, however, investment orders will begin to decrease as indicated by the equation $I = m(B_0 + A) - nK$ and the stability of investment activity will be disturbed.

During the depression the process described here is reversed. Investment orders are not sufficient to cover the replacement requirements; this leads to a decrease in the volume of capital equipment and eventually to a resumption of the increase in investment orders. To stabilize investment activity at a level lower than that which provides adequate replacement is as impossible as to stabilize it at a level which exceeds the replacement requirements.

3. We shall now make a detailed examination of the way in which the mechanism of the trade cycle functions. Fig. 1.4 shows deviations from the average for: investment orders I, the production of investment goods equal to the gross accumulation A, deliveries of new equipment D, i.e. the values: $I - I_0$, $A - A_0$, $D - D_0$. It should be remembered that the averages I_0, A_0, and

D_0 are all equal and that they are also equal to the replacement requirements U.

Conclusion (*a*) at the beginning of this section shows that the curve A is shifted approximately by $\frac{1}{2}\vartheta$ and the curve D by ϑ from the curve I.

The ordinate of the curve D is equal to $D-D_0$ which, as shown by conclusion (*c*), is also equal to the change per unit of

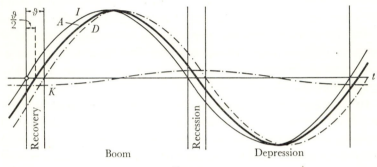

FIG. 1.4

time in the volume of capital equipment K. On this basis the curve K can be drawn. The curve K will rise during the period when the ordinate of the curve D is positive and it will decline when the ordinate of the curve D is negative. (Also in this case the abscissa axis is taken to correspond to the average value of K which is denoted by K_0, i.e. deviations from the average $K-K_0$ are again presented here).

By *recovery* we understand here the phase of the cycle of the length ϑ during which investment orders exceed the level of replacement requirements; capital equipment, however, has not yet begun to expand because deliveries of new equipment are as yet lower than the replacement requirements.

The production of investment goods A, which is equal to the gross accumulation, increases; but the volume of equipment K is still shrinking, as a result of which investment orders I which are equal to $m(B_0-A)-nK$ rise steeply.

During the *boom* deliveries of new equipment already exceed the replacement requirements and consequently capital equipment K begins to expand. The increase of K initially restrains the rate of growth of investment orders and subsequently causes their decline. This is followed in the second half of the boom by a decline in the production of investment goods.

During the *recession* investment orders are below the level of replacement requirements. The volume of capital equipment, however, is still expanding because deliveries of new equipment are higher than this level.

The production of investment goods which is equal to the gross accumulation A continues to fall, and this together with the increase of K, produces a steep fall in investment orders.

During the *depression* deliveries of new equipment are already below the level of replacement requirements, and consequently the volume of capital equipment K shrinks. This decrease in K initially slows down the fall in investment orders and subsequently causes their increase. This is followed by a rise in the production of investment goods in the second half of the depression.

4. We considered here the interrelated changes of investment orders, the gross accumulation, and the volume of capital equipment which produce the business cycle. The fluctuations of the gross accumulation which result from this mechanism must also be reflected in the fluctuations of the aggregate production. The gross real profits P are, on the one hand, an increasing function of the gross accumulation A (P is proportionate to $B_0 + A$, where B_0 is the constant part of capitalists' consumption), and on the other hand, they can be expressed as the product of the volume of the aggregate production and of the profit per unit of output.†

The relation between changes in the gross accumulation which is equal to the production of investment goods, and those of the aggregate production materialises in the following way.

† We assume here that aggregate production and profit per unit of output rise or fall together, which is actually the case. This results at least to some extent from the fact that a part of wages are overheads.

When production of investment goods rises the aggregate production increases directly *pro tanto*, but in addition there is an increase due to the demand for consumer goods on the part of the workers newly engaged in the investment goods industries. The consequent increase in employment in the consumer-goods industries leads to a further rise in the demand for consumer goods. The levels of aggregate production and of the profit per unit of output will ultimately rise to such an extent that the increment in real profits is equated to the increment of the production of investment goods.

The account of the process is not yet complete because changes in capitalists' consumption have not been taken into consideration. This consumption C is dependent to a certain degree on the aggregate profits P and will increase together with the gross accumulation A since from equation (1.2) and (1.3) it follows that $C = (B_0 + \lambda A)/(1 - \lambda)$. The increase in capitalists' consumption exerts the same influence as that in the production of investment goods: the production of consumer goods for capitalists expands; this leads to an increase in employment and this raises again the demand for consumer goods for the workers which causes a further rise in production. *The aggregate production and the profit per unit of output will ultimately rise to such an extent as to assure an increment in real profits equal to that of production of investment goods and capitalists' consumption.*

5. Some doubts may be raised by the final part of the preceding paragraph. The conclusion that the increase in capitalists' consumption increases in turn their profits, contradicts the common conviction, that the more is consumed the less is saved. This approach, which is correct with regard to a single capitalist, does not apply to the capitalist class as a whole. If some capitalists spend money, either on investment or consumer goods, their money passes to other capitalists in the form of profits. Investment or consumption of some capitalists creates profits for others. Capitalists as a class gain exactly as much as they invest or consume, and if—in a closed system—they ceased to construct and consume they could not make any money at all.

Thus capitalists, as a whole, determine their own profits by the extent of their investment and personal consumption. In a way they are 'masters of their fate'; but how they 'master' it is determined by objective factors, so that fluctuations of profits appear after all to be unavoidable. Capitalists' consumption is a function of the gross accumulation. The gross accumulation which is equal to the production of investment goods is determined by investment orders which in turn were undertaken in a past period on the basis of the profitability in that period, i.e. on the basis of the gross accumulation and the volume of capital equipment in that period.

The question may still arise, where the capitalists find the 'means' to increase the production of investment goods or their personal consumption. If we abstract from the 'technical' elements of the money market, we may say that the capitalists as a whole do not need money in order to achieve this since, as shown above, the expenditure of some capitalists is converted into profits for others; the outlay on construction of a fixed asset is by no means 'frozen', as some people think, and 'released' only as the capital invested is gradually written off—but it is already returned in the course of construction in the form of profits accruing to the firms whose sales (either of investment or consumer goods) are directly or indirectly connected with this construction. If during a particular period more money is spent, e.g. out of bank deposits, then *pro tanto* more money flows back into the banks in the form of realised profits, so that the sum of deposits remains unchanged. In actual fact, however, credit inflation is inevitable owing to the 'technical' elements of the money market mentioned above. This is connected with the fact discussed above that the increase in production of investment goods or in the capitalists' consumption, i.e. in real profits, must be reflected in the increase in aggregate production. This increase (together with the usual rise of prices which accompanies it) engenders a higher demand for money in circulation i.e. cash and current accounts, which is met by credit inflation.

Thus the demand for money in circulation increases during the upswing and falls during the downswing. The rise and fall in the rate of interest follows suit. This is the basis of our assumption that the rate of interest i is an increasing function of the gross profitability P/K (which is only a crude approximation). This assumption enables us to pass from equation (1.7):

$$\frac{I}{K} = f\left(\frac{P}{K}, i\right) \qquad (1.7)$$

where f is an increasing function of P/K and a decreasing function of i, to the equation (1.8):

$$\frac{I}{K} = F\left(\frac{P}{K}\right) \qquad (1.8)$$

Moreover, we assumed that i rises sufficiently slowly in relation to the gross profitability P/K for the stimulating effect o the increase in the latter upon investment to outweigh the restraining influence of the rise in the rate of interest i. If this rate were to increase sufficiently fast for the influence of the increase in gross profitability to be fully offset, an upswing would prove impossible. There is thus a close connection between the phenomenon of the business cycle, and the response of the banking system to the increase in demand for money in circulation at a rate of interest which is not prohibitive to the rise in investment.

2. ON FOREIGN TRADE AND 'DOMESTIC EXPORTS'

[1934]

1. Capturing a new foreign market is frequently mentioned as a way out of depression. But it is usually not added that what is essential in this context is an increase in the export surplus rather than in absolute exports.

In fact, aggregate profits are equal to capitalists' consumption *plus* investment *plus* the balance of foreign trade.† Profits of a given year were either consumed, invested in construction of capital equipment and in increase in inventories or, finally, were used for repayment of foreign debts or granting of foreign credits.‡ In the course of a 'normal' upswing the increase in profits is due to the rise of the component 'investment'. Let us suppose that eight factories are built each year instead of five. The real income of the capitalists—if other components of profits remain constant —increases by the value of these three 'additional' factories.§ The expansion of investment activity must therefore lead to such a rise in aggregate production and in the profit per unit of output that this increase in aggregate profits would materialize. The consequent higher profitability of existing establishments induces a further rise in investment activity which thus enhances the upswing.

In order to stimulate the upswing by means of foreign trade, the balance of trade component of profits must increase, i.e. new surplus of exports over imports must be achieved.

† We abstract from workers' savings here.
‡ In addition to the increase of foreign claims or the payments of foreign debts the influx of gold may also be an equivalent of the surplus of exports over imports. Gold influx, however, may be treated in the same way as that of foreign currency, i.e. as an increase in foreign claims.
§ We assume—as is actually the case—that increased investment is carried out by means of creation of purchasing power rather than at the expense of capitalists' consumption.

15

This surplus, like a boom in investment activity, leads to such a general increase in production and in the profit per unit of output that aggregate profits rise by an amount equal to the increment of the balance of trade. The higher profitability of existing establishments, which results from this, acts as a stimulus to investment activity; the upswing resulting from a new surplus in foreign trade thus leads to a 'normal' boom.

But if exports increase and at the same time there is an equal increase in imports, overall profits remain unchanged; international trade is boosted, but production in the country considered does not increase, nor will there be any inducement for expansion of investment activity. If, e.g. Great Britain increases its exports to China this would lead to an improvement in the British economic situation if China pays for these imports in gold or if she receives a loan from British capitalists which will be ultimately used for the purchase of British goods. The profits of British capitalists will then be increased by the amount equal to the new surplus in trade with China. But if more machines were exported to China, and *pro tanto* more cotton cloth were imported from China, then the situation in the British machine industry would improve, and the situation in the British cotton industry would deteriorate, while the general economic situation would remain unchanged since the aggregate profits would not have increased.

2. Let us assume that increased exports from a given country do involve a rise in the surplus of foreign trade. The condition for stimulating the upswing is thus fulfilled—an increase in the balance of trade is followed by a rise in production. The latter, however, leads, *inter alia*, to a greater demand for foreign commodities, especially raw materials, which are an indispensable element of domestic production—and thus to an increase in imports.†

---

† As a result of the price increase accompanying the upswing imports will increase and exports will slacken, owing to a weakening in the competitive position of the country's products. This factor plays a considerably lesser role than the increased demand for foreign goods resulting from the rise in production. Thus, for the sake of simplicity, we shall not take it into account here.

On foreign trade

Let us denote the increase in the balance of trade by s, the corresponding increase in imports and exports by i and e respectively. Thus we obtain:

$$e = i + s \qquad (2.1)$$

This means that exports must increase not only by the increment of the balance of trade but also by an additional amount which would warrant a rise in imports, indispensable for the expansion of production. In other words: only a part of the total increase in exports contributes to the increase in the balance of trade and consequently in aggregate profits. The remainder is used for additional imports necessary for the higher output.

We shall now establish the relation between the increments i and s. As was shown above, the increase in the balance of trade by s raises aggregate profits *pro tanto*. Let the relative share of profits in the aggregate value of production be α:† thus production will increase by s/α. Moreover let the ratio of imports to the value of aggregate production be β;‡ then the increase in imports will be $i = \beta(s/\alpha)$; thus we obtain:

$$\frac{s}{i} = \frac{e-i}{i} = \frac{\alpha}{\beta} \qquad (2.2)$$

We shall illustrate this process by an example. If some country manages to increase the balance of trade and its total exports increase by 70 mil. zl., only a part of this sum raises the balance of trade, while another part is used to cover the imports of goods indispensable for the expansion of production. The proportion between these two parts is the same as that between the relative share of profits in the value of aggregate production (equal, say, to 0·5), and the ratio of imports to this value (equal, say, to 0·2). It follows that the increase of the balance of trade amounts to

$$\frac{0 \cdot 5}{0 \cdot 5 + 0 \cdot 2}\, 70 = 50 \text{ mil. zl.}$$

† This relative share changes in the course of the business cycle, increasing during the upswing and declining during the downswing. However, the changes are rather small, and for the sake of simplicity it will be treated as constant here.

‡ This ratio is of course, subject to changes which, however, are not of great importance and for the sake of simplicity it will be treated as constant here.

Exports rise additionally to 20 mil. zl. but imports increase by the same amount, or exports increase by 70 mil. zl., imports by 20 mil. zl., and the balance rises by 50 mil. zl., and the aggregate profits by just as much.

3. If a government borrows from the capitalists at home, spending the proceeds of the loan, e.g. on armaments, payment of doles, or public works, the result is very similar to that of securing a surplus in foreign trade. To the surplus of exports over imports there corresponds here the sale of commodities, used for the purposes mentioned above: armaments, consumer goods for the unemployed; construction materials for public works and consumer goods for the workers employed in these works. The equivalent of these sales of commodities is the increase in the claims of the capitalists on their government, just as the equivalent of the surplus achieved in foreign trade was the increase of foreign claims or the reduction of foreign debts. And obviously this increase in government debts may absorb profits in the same way as an increase in foreign claims (or a fall in foreign debts). Consequently the formula for profits must be modified: in addition to capitalists' consumption, investment and the balance of trade, they also include 'domestic exports', equal to the increase of government indebtedness to capitalists. The starting of 'domestic exports' thus stimulates the upswing in the same way as a surplus secured in foreign trade. It is followed by such an increase in production and in the profit per unit of output that a rise in aggregate profits takes place which is equal to these 'exports'. This in turn acts as a stimulus for the expansion of investment activity. Financial processes connected with securing a surplus in foreign trade and with 'domestic exports' are also very similar in character.

The analogy is obvious in the case when the capitalists of a given country grant a foreign loan or a loan to their government which is used for purchase of commodities in that country. The capitalists lend money abroad or to their government in return for bonds. Funds obtained by a foreign country or by the government flow back through the purchases of commodities to the capitalists, if we abstract from workers' savings (though, of course, not necessarily to the same capitalists). As a result, the profits of the capitalist class in a given period increase by an amount equal to the value of the government or foreign bonds received, which is equal in turn to the surplus secured in foreign trade or to 'domestic exports' respectively.

A surplus in foreign trade may also be covered by the influx to the country considered of foreign currency or gold rather than by its granting foreign loans. In the case of 'domestic exports' the analogous process is, as will be shown below, the financing of government expenditure by the Central Bank.

Gold and foreign currency which are the equivalent of the surplus in foreign trade will be ultimately exchanged by capitalists for national currency at the Central Bank or used to repay credits extended to them by this bank. The profits of capitalists will rise in a given period by the amount of the increase in the circulation of notes and of the repayment of credits to the Central Bank which is equal to the surplus secured in foreign trade.

If 'domestic exports' are financed by discounting treasury bills in the Central Bank, the notes acquired by the government pass into the hands of capitalists. These notes either remain in circulation or are ultimately used for repayment of credits to the Central Bank. The profits of capitalists increase in a given period by the sum of the increase in the quantity of money in circulation and of the repayment of credits to the Central Bank which sum is equal to the 'domestic exports'.

In either case the profits of capitalists are raised by the sum of the increase in the quantity of money in circulation and of the reduction in the Central Bank credits.

The foreign claims of the Central Bank in the form of gold or foreign currency or its claims on the government in the form of treasury bills increase by the same amount. In this way foreign countries or the government become indebted to the capitalists of a given country through the medium of the Central Bank to the extent of the surplus secured in foreign trade or of the 'domestic exports'.

4. As a result of the stimulation of the upswing through 'domestic exports'—just as in the case of the application of any other device for this purpose—a rise in imports will take place due to the increased demand for foreign goods which are indispensable for home production (see section 2 of this chapter). Since there was no reason for a simultaneous increase in exports, 'domestic exports' are accompanied by a decrease of the balance of trade. Let us examine the problem in detail with reference to the argument of section 2.

We shall denote the increase in imports by i, as above, and the increase in the balance of trade by s. Since exports are assumed to be unchanged

$$i = -s \qquad (2.3)$$

which means that the rise in imports equals the decrease in the balance of trade. We shall denote 'domestic exports' per unit of time by e_1. It was shown in the preceding section that as a result of stimulating the upswing by means of 'domestic exports', the profits of capitalists increase by e_1. However, we did not take into account how this affects the balance of foreign trade. If this balance changes by s, then according to the argument in section 1, profits change by s as well. Thus the total increase in profits is $e_1 + s$. And since $s = -i$ here, the increase in profits will amount to $e_1 - i$, i.e. they will be equal to the difference between 'domestic exports' and the rise in imports as a result of the stimulating effect of 'domestic exports' upon aggregate production.

As in section 2, we shall now denote the share of profits in the value of aggregate production by α; thus the value of production will increase by $(e_1 - i)/\alpha$. If, moreover, we denote the ratio of imports to the value of aggregate production by β, the corresponding rise in imports will amount to $i = [(e_1 - i)/\alpha]\,\beta$. It follows that

$$\frac{e_1 - i}{i} = \frac{\alpha}{\beta} \qquad (2.4)$$

This equation is identical with the equation (2.2) except that instead of the increase in exports e, we have here the 'domestic exports' e_1. Like the equation (2.2) the equation (2.4) indicates that 'domestic exports' are divided into two parts $e_1 - i$ and i bearing the same relation as α to β (where α is the relative share of profits in the value of aggregate production, and β the ratio of imports to the value of aggregate production). The part $e_1 - i$ is equal to the increase in profits and the part i to the rise in imports. But it is here that a fundamental difference arises: both the increase in 'foreign exports' and the increase in 'domestic exports' lead to a rise in aggregate profits by $e - i$ or $e_1 - i$; but, while part i of the increase in 'foreign exports' actually *covers* the growth of imports by means of international trade, the part i of 'domestic exports' is equal to the increase in imports only in an *arithmetical* sense and, of course, is not *convertible* into imports. This brings out the fact that 'domestic exports' lead to a deterioration in the balance of trade.

We can illustrate these processes by an example. Let us assume that the government borrowed in the free market or from the Central Bank 70 mil. zl. and spent it on public works. As a result of the increase in production, imports increase by i, which—the level of exports remaining unchanged—means a reduction in the balance of trade by the same amount. Profits rise by $70 - i$. This item bears the same proportion to i as the relative share of profits in the value of aggregate production (say 0·5) to the ratio of imports to the aggregate production (say 0·2). It follows that the rise in imports, and thus the fall in the balance of trade, amounts to 20 mil. zl. This rise in imports will have two results: (1) profits will increase not by 70, but only by 50 mil. zl.; (2) there will be a deterioration of 20 mil. zl. in the balance of trade.

5. It was shown in the preceding section that the starting of 'domestic exports' leads to a fall in the balance of trade. In the balance of payments this can be covered by: (1) the influx of foreign capital; (2) the suspension of the servicing of foreign debts; (3) outflow of gold and foreign currency. Since 'domestic exports' raise the average profitability, there will be a tendency for the influx of foreign capital into the country which, how-

ever, is usually offset by the anxieties as to the solvency of the country raised among foreign capitalists by the deterioration of the balance of trade. As foreign investment is not forthcoming, gold and foreign currency begin in fact to flow out of the country.

This can still be prevented (in the case of a debtor's country) by suspending the servicing of foreign debts. If however, 'domestic exports' exceed a certain level, the balance of foreign trade—as a result of a substantial rise in production and im-ports—becomes nevertheless negative, and gold or foreign currency start again to flow out of the country. Finally reserves of foreign currency and gold decline to such an extent that the only way to maintain imports is to try to increase exports through currency devaluation.

As a result of devaluation the prices of domestic products in terms of foreign exchange are reduced which leads to such an increase in their exports that, despite the unfavourable terms of trade, it is possible to purchase for the proceeds from exports a higher volume of foreign goods. In this way the imports required for the production, increased as a result of starting the 'domestic exports', are secured. There is, however, a limit to securing imports in this way. First of all the reduction of domestic prices in terms of foreign currency is limited, both as to the magnitude and the time it lasts, by a tendency of these prices to rise in terms of the domestic currency. But even if we abstract from this tendency—which can be prevented, e.g. in such a way that no formal devaluation of currency is undertaken but only a general export premium is established—the capacity to secure imports is, nevertheless, limited. Let us suppose that the prices for the products of a given country are reduced n times by currency devaluation, and that, as a result, the volume of exports increases m times: the imports of foreign goods, acquired in exchange for these exports, will thus change in the proportion m/n. It is obvious that for sufficiently large values of n the ratio m/n will become less than one, i.e. for a larger quantity of domestic products a smaller quantity of foreign goods than before the currency devaluation will be obtained. Thus, there is a certain maximum level of imports which can be secured through devaluation. The devaluation of currency beyond this point will lead, not to a rise, but to a fall in the capacity of a given country to import. This also shows that stimulating the upswing by means of 'domestic exports' has a limit: the aggregate production cannot reach such a level that indispensable imports would be greater than the maximum imports obtainable through devaluation. This may, and often will result in a situation in which the upswing caused by 'domestic exports' will not lead to the full utilization of idle capital equipment because of the deficiency of foreign goods (especially raw materials) which are an indispensable complementary factor. The more a given economy depends on imports, and the more difficult it is for this economy to expand its exports through devaluation (e.g. in view of the raising of custom duties by other countries), the sooner will the upswing engendered by 'domestic exports' reach its peak.

It should be added that with progressing devaluation the real income reaches its maximum at an earlier point than production; for a decreasing amount of real income is yielded by a unit of aggregate production, a part of this production being exchanged for foreign goods at deteriorating terms of trade.

6. We concentrated above on the phase of stimulating the upswing by a surplus secured in foreign trade or by 'domestic exports'. The resulting increase in profits induces an expansion of investment activity and in this way the phase of the 'natural' boom is reached.

Thus it is possible then to reduce gradually the 'domestic exports', slowing down the progress of the upswing without, however, causing a collapse of the boom. If the upswing is stimulated through a rise in the balance of trade this influence is automatically halted in the period of increasing investment. Indeed, the latter leads to an expansion of production and thus to a rise in imports which is not counterbalanced by an increase in exports (investment activity has much the same effect here as 'domestic exports'). This leads to a deterioration in the balance of trade whose increase had previously stimulated the upswing, and at a certain level of production the difficulties which were discussed in the preceding section may appear. By means of calculations similar to those in sections 2 and 4 of this chapter, it is possible to estimate the level of investment at which a tension in the balance of trade may arise.

Let us denote by s the increase in the balance of trade which caused the upswing. Let us suppose that in the next phase of the upswing investment increased by k, and the previous increase in the balance of trade got 'lost' owing to the increase in imports, i.e. it dropped by s thus returning to its initial level. Therefore in the period of expansion of investment, aggregate profits increased because of the rise in the item 'investment' by k, but fell by s as a result of the decline in the item 'balance of trade'. On balance the increase in profits amounted to $k-s$. As in sections 2 and 4, let us denote the relative share of profits in the value of aggregate production by α and the ratio of imports to this value by β. The increase in the value of production corresponding to the increase in profits by $k-s$ is equal to $(k-s)/\alpha$, and the corresponding rise in imports to $[(k-s)/\alpha]\beta$. Since imports increased by the same amount as the decline in the balance of trade, i.e. by s, we obtain:

$$\frac{k-s}{\alpha}\beta = s$$

It follows directly that $k = s\left(1+\dfrac{\alpha}{\beta}\right)$ (1.5)

As in sections 2 and 4, let $\alpha = 0.5$ and $\beta = 0.2$; k will then amount to $3.5\,s$. It will be seen that the tension in the balance of payments, which accompanied 'domestic exports' from the start, in the case of an upswing stimulated by securing a surplus in foreign trade arises only at the point when investment has reached a level several times greater than this surplus, i.e. at an advanced stage of the boom. Moreover, it is probable that prior to this a considerable improvement in the economic situation which does not involve balance of payment difficulties will lead to an influx of foreign capital. If this flow of foreign capital is lasting in character there may be no tension in the balance of payments at a later stage as well. It is now clear what are the advantages of an upswing stimulated by means of securing a surplus in foreign trade. It is worth mentioning that the 'natural' upswing based on the automatic increase in investment activity does not enjoy these advantages, and if there is no influx of foreign capital, it will be confronted with the same balance of payments difficulties as the upswing based on 'domestic exports'.

3. THE MECHANISM OF THE
BUSINESS UPSWING

[1935]

1. Mass unemployment seems to be the most obvious symptom of depression. Is this unemployment due to the shortage of capital equipment, i.e. to inadequate accumulation of fixed capital in relation to the increase of population? Certainly not. The position is rather the reverse. During the depression the existing capital equipment is utilized to a small degree: the idle capital equipment is the counterpart of the unemployed labour force. To what should be attributed the fact that the owner of unutilized equipment who encounters a lasting supply of idle labour does not embark upon production? Any single entrepreneur would certainly answer that this would be an unprofitable proposition: the prices at which he could sell would not even cover his current costs, i.e. the outlay on raw materials, labour, taxes, etc. Thus a reduction of wages is being recommended as a way to overcome the depression. Now, one of the main features of the capitalist system is the fact that what is to the advantage of a single entrepreneur does not necessarily benefit all entrepreneurs as a class. If one entrepreneur reduces wages he is able *ceteris paribus* to expand production; but once all entrepreneurs do the same thing—the result will be entirely different.

Let us assume that wages have been in fact generally reduced, and likewise taxes as a counterpart of cuts in civil servants' salaries. Now the entrepreneurs owing to the 'improved' price–wage relation utilize their equipment to capacity and in consequence unemployment vanishes. Has depression been thus overcome? By no means, as the goods produced have still to be

26

sold. Now, production has risen considerably and as a result of an increase in the price–wage relation the part of production equivalent to profits (including depreciation) of the capitalists (entrepreneurs and rentiers) has grown even more. A precondition for an equilibrium at this new higher level is that this part of production which is not consumed by workers or by civil servants should be acquired by capitalists for their increased profits; in other words, the capitalists must spend immediately all their additional profits on consumption or investment. It is, however, most unlikely that this should in fact happen. Capitalists' consumption changes in general but little in the course of the business cycle. It is true that increased profitability stimulates investment but this stimulus will not work right away since the entrepreneurs will temporise until they are convinced that the higher profitability is going to last. Therefore the immediate effect of increased profits will be an accumulation of money reserves in the hands of entrepreneurs and in the banks. Then, however, the goods which are the equivalent of the increased profits will remain unsold. The accumulating stocks will sound the alarm for a new price reduction of goods which do not find any outlet. Thus the effect of the cost reduction will be cancelled. On balance only a price reduction will have occured, offsetting the advantage of the cost reduction to the entrepreneurs since unemployment going hand in hand with under-utilization of equipment will reappear.

In fact wage reduction does not, as a rule, result even in the temporary increase in production described above. Indeed, not only investment but even utilization of existing equipment will not respond immediately to an improvement in profitability. For immediately after the reduction of wages and before the entrepreneurs manage to increase production within the existing capital equipment a fall in prices makes its appearance. As the entrepreneurs do not at once make use of the means taken away from the workers for buying consumption or investment goods, the revenue of industry is reduced *pro tanto*. What the entrepreneurs gain on wage reductions is soon dissipated through price declines. All this could be noticed in all countries during the world depression in the period 1931–2, when the wave of wage reductions brought about a rapid fall in prices rather than an increase in production.

2. The doctrine of wage cuts as the way out of depression is sometimes supplemented by a remedy against the price fall. Creation of cartels is recommended to stop the 'cut throat competition'. Let us assume that in all industries cartels have been formed, that wages have been duly reduced, but that the diminished demand of the workers could not have any repercussions on prices since they are maintained by cartels at a stable level. Will the 'improved' price–wage relation be of any help in overcoming the depression? Now, it is rather unlikely that cartels would invest profits derived by wage reductions more promptly than the entrepreneurs under conditions of 'free competition'. The opposite is rather the case. Thus in a totally cartelized system, just as under 'free competition', the proceeds of industry will diminish as much as their costs, and as prices remain unchanged the sales of goods will drop in the same proportion as the proceeds have shrunk. Thus while wage reductions do not cause any increase in production in the case of a competitive economy, in a fully cartelized system they lead, as a result of rigidity of prices, to a shrinkage of production and a rise in unemployment.

In a 'mixed' system, consisting of a cartelized and a competitive sector, the result of wage cuts will be something intermediate: a fall of production will ensue but it will be weaker than in a fully cartelized system.

3. It follows from the above argument that a reduction of wages does not constitute a way out of depression, because the gains are not used immediately by the capitalists for purchase of investment goods. Now we shall try to prove that the opposite is the case: the increase in investment *per se* unaccompanied by a wage reduction causes a rise in output.

Let us assume that as a result of some important invention there is an increase in investment associated with its spreading.

Now, is it possible for the capitalists to step up their investment, even though their profits have not increased (there was no reduction in wages) nor have they curtailed their consumption *ad hoc* (this, indeed, is most unlikely). The financing of additional investment is effected by the so called creation of purchasing power. The demand for bank credits increases and these are granted by the banks. The means used by the entrepreneurs for construction of new establishments reach the industries of investment goods. This additional demand makes for setting to work idle equipment and unemployed labour. The increased employment is a source of additional demand for consumer goods and thus results in turn in higher employment in the respective industries. Finally the additional investment outlay finds its way directly and through the workers' spending into the pockets of capitalists (we assume that workers do not save). The additional profits flow back as deposits to the banks. Bank credits increase by the amount additionally invested and deposits by the amount of additional profits. The entrepreneurs who engage in additional investment are 'propelling' into the pockets of other capitalists profits which are equal to their investment, and they are becoming indebted to these capitalists to the same extent *via* banks.

In the preceding sections we were faced with the problem whether the profits resulting from the reduction of costs are invested. In the case presently considered, the profits, to put it paradoxically, are invested even before they come into being. Profits that are not invested cannot be retained because they are annihilated by the ensuing fall in production and prices. The creation of the purchasing power for financing additional investment increases the output from the low level reached in the depression and thus creates profits equal to this investment.

It should be pointed out that the increase in output will result in an increased demand for money in circulation, and thus will call for a rise in credits of the Central Bank. Should the Bank respond to it by raising the rate of interest to a level at which total investment would decline by the amount equal to the additional investment caused by the new invention, no increase in investment would ensue and the economic situation would not improve. Therefore the precondition for the upswing is that the rate of interest should not increase too much in response to an increased demand for cash.

What will happen, however, when the new invention has been spread and the original source of the business upswing has dried up and thus the stimulus for investment vanishes? Is the downswing unavoidable then? No, because in the meantime the increased profitability prevailing in the economy as a whole will have resulted in a rise in investment. It is this investment caused by higher profitability which will step in when the effect of the new invention will have petered out.

4. We described in the preceding section a business upswing resulting from the investment stimulated by an important invention, which to some extent is a matter of chance. Without such an external stimulus, would the depression last for ever? Is it not inherent in the depression to breed forces that put an end to it by causing an increase in investment?

Let us assume that the economy became stabilized at the bottom of the depression at a very low level of economic activity; that investment in particular has shrunk to such a degree that it does not cover the necessary replacement of the ageing capital equipment. Let us suppose that this equipment consists of 2000 establishments and that every year 100 of them get out of use, but only 60 establishments are constructed. Thus the capital equipment shrinks every year by 40 establishments. However, it is this destruction of equipment that after a rather prolonged period initiates a business upswing. For owing to the shrinkage of capital equipment the same demand is met by a declining number of existing establishments which as a result improve their degree of utilization. Once the profitability of the existing capital equipment has thus increased, the level of investment will increase as well. The finance for it will be provided—as was described in the preceding section—by creation of additional purchasing power. This will result in an increase of the output of investment goods and of employment in the respective branches of industry. Moreover, the rise in demand on the part of the newly-employed workers for consumption goods will cause fuller employment in the consumer-good industries. This general increase in production brings about a further rise in profitability, followed by a new expansion of investment activity, a new creation of purchasing power, etc.

This is, indeed, a cumulative process causing a steady upswing. However, once investment starts to exceed the level of necessary replacement of fixed capital, i.e. once more establishments are constructed per year than the 100 establishments which are scrapped—then the factors hampering the upswing make their appearance. Just as during the depression the shrinkage of capital equipment was the inception of the upswing, so now the expansion of this equipment finally brings the boom to a stop and starts the downswing.

The process of collapse of the boom is the reverse of that starting the upswing from the bottom of depression. Let us assume that at the top of the boom investment is stabilized at the level of 140 establishments and, as 100 establishments are scrapped p.a., the capital equipment is expanding by 40 establishments p.a. Now the demand will be met by an increasing number of establishments and as a result the degree of utilization of each of them will diminish. The resulting lower profitability will be followed by a decline in investment. And just as the increase in investment at the bottom of depression meant the start of the upswing of production and of a decline in unemployment—a fall in production and an increase in unemployment will ensue here. And this downward movement will gather momentum as in the period of the upswing the upward tendencies were cumulative in character.

It is not, of course, the purpose of this essay to present a complete theory of business fluctuations. An attempt is made to give a general idea of the mechanism of a 'natural' upswing, and in particular to clarify one of its aspects. It now becomes apparent that investment has a favourable effect upon the economic situation only at the time when it is executed and provides an outlet for additional purchasing power. On the other hand the productive character of investment contributes to the slackening of the upswing and finally brings it to an end. For it is the expansion of capital equipment that in the light of the above analysis causes the collapse of the boom. We face here one of the most remarkable paradoxes of the capitalist system. The expansion of the capital equipment, i.e. the increase in the national wealth, contains the seed of a depression in the course of which the additional wealth proves to be only potential in character. For a considerable part of capital equipment is idle then and becomes useful only in the next upswing.

This statement sheds some light on the problem of government anti-slump intervention by means of public investment, with which we shall deal now.

5. After we have studied the mechanism of the business cycle let us turn again to the case where the upswing is started by a new invention which stimulates some entrepreneurs to embark upon 'extra investment'. By making use for this purpose of additional purchasing power, they set in motion the mechanism of the upswing. This case is very close to that of government anti-slump intervention. In order to pass from the former to the latter it suffices to substitute for the entrepreneurs induced to invest by the new invention the government taking up investment which is financed likewise by means of additional purchasing power in order to break the deadlock of the slump.

Let us assume that the government issues treasury bills and sells them to the banks. The government spends the money, e.g. on construction of railways. As in the cases described above, employment in investment-good industries increases and subsequently, as a result of the higher purchasing power of the workers, in consumption-good industries as well. The amounts spent by the government flow as profits directly or through spending of the workers into the pockets of capitalists, and return to the banks as their deposits. On the side of bank assets, the government debt accrues in the form of discounted bills, on the side of liabilities there is an increase in deposits equal to the additional profits. Thus the government gets indebted via banks to the private capitalists by an amount equal to the value of the investment effected. It will be seen that a complete analogy exists between the case now being considered and that of an upswing resulting from a new invention. And in both instances increased profitability of the industry as a whole will stimulate investment and thus enhance the upswing which as a result will continue even if the government gradually reduces its investment activity. Thus an upswing started by a new invention continues after its impact has spent itself.

It should be emphasized that the pattern of public investment taken up is not essential for the effect of government intervention; what matters is that investment should be financed by additional purchasing power. The creation of purchasing power for the sake of financing the budget deficit, whatever its reason, renders a similar effect. The divergence consists only in that the additional purchasing power flows initially into different industries. Let us assume, for instance, that the amount derived from discounting treasury bills is used for the payment of doles. In this case the direct effect of government intervention will be felt in consumer-good industries. Only after some time, when their increased profitability will induce them to invest, will prosperity be shared by investment-good industries as well. This increased investment activity financed by creation of purchasing power will enhance the upswing, so that the latter will continue even after the budget deficits will have vanished—owing to the increase in tax revenues resulting from the rise in incomes and sales.

Thus after some time private investment 'takes over' from public investment: the 'artificial' prosperity is replaced by a 'natural' one which, by the way, sooner or later—as was proved in the preceding chapter—will come to a stop as a result of expansion of capital equipment.

It must be added that the pre-condition of successful government intervention—and of the natural upswing as well—is the possibility of meeting the increased demand for credits by the banking system without increasing the rate of interest too much. Should the rate of interest increase to such an extent that private investment is curtailed by exactly the amount of government borrowing—then obviously no purchasing power would be created, but only a shift in its structure would take place.

4. A THEORY OF COMMODITY, INCOME AND CAPITAL TAXATION

[1937]

In this paper we shall consider the effects of commodity taxes, income taxes, and capital taxes on employment, national income and its distribution—with capital equipment and money wages given. The first condition confines our analysis to the short period; the second is merely a simplification which can be avoided by measuring the values not in money terms, but in wage units. In addition we make the following simplifying assumptions:

(1) That we are considering a closed economic system with a surplus of all types of labour and equipment;

(2) That workers spend all they receive as wages or doles (for unemployment, disability, etc.) and, thus, that only capitalists (entrepreneurs and rentiers) save; and

(3) That the State Budget is balanced, all State expenditure being financed by taxation.†

We make also in the course of the argument some additional assumptions of more special character.

Our argument is divided into four stages. In the first stage we briefly consider short-period equilibrium in an economy without taxation and State expenditure, and in the subsequent stages introduce commodity taxes, income taxes, and capital taxes. We assume the commodity tax to be levied only on wage-goods and the income tax only on capitalists' income.

---

† It is quite simple to pass from this to the more general case of an unbalanced budget, superimposing on our results the effects of State borrowing or repayment of debts.

1. We shall mean by gross profit from an enterprise the difference between the value of sales and prime costs. It is this quantity which is maximised when the output of the enterprise corresponds to the point of intersection of the marginal prime cost and the marginal revenue curve. National income we shall call (as Keynes does) the sum of all gross profits and of the wage bill. On the other hand, national income is also the value of total consumption and investment. Since the workers are supposed to consume all they earn, the total gross profit P must be equal to capitalists' consumption C_c plus investment I:

$$P = C_c + I$$

If the sum of the expenditure of capitalists on consumption and investment $C_c + I$ increases (or decreases), a shift of the marginal revenue curves takes place, and employment is 'pushed' to the point at which total gross profit P is equal to the increased (or decreased) sum of spending for capitalists' consumption and investment.

It is clear that the above equation is equivalent (on our assumption that workers do not save) to the equality of savings S and investment I, for by subtracting C_c from both sides we attain: $S = I$.

As we see, the total gross profit P is determined by the rate of investment I—which is equal to the capitalists' saving S—and by their propensity to consume. We make now some plausible assumptions as to these determinants of gross profit. We assume that if some change in basic data occurs:

(1) The rate of investment I does not change *immediately*, because it is the result of previous investment decisions requiring a certain not very short time for completion;

(2) The capitalists' propensity to consume is insensitive to the expectations of the change in income, and it is only the actual rise (or fall) in income which can induce them to raise (or to lower) their standard of living.

It follows from these assumptions that the gross profit $P = C_c + I$ can be altered by the change of basic conditions only with a certain time-lag, and one which is not very short. For in the meantime the rate of investment I remains unaltered, while the capitalists' propensity to consume is not affected by the expectations of the change in their income.

2. Let us now introduce into our system State expenditure financed by wage-goods taxation. The Government spends money either for officials' salaries or for the doles of the un-employed, disabled, etc. The tax is regarded, for the sake of simplicity, as being reckoned *ad valorem* at a constant rate for all kinds of wage-goods. It is obvious that this type of tax consti-tutes a new kind of prime cost.

The national income is now equal to the sum of gross profits, workers' wages, and taxes imposed on wage-goods. On the other hand, the national income is equal to the value of total con-sumption and investment. Now, the workers' wages are equal to the value of their consumption. The sum of taxes is equal to the sum of salaries of officials and doles, which are also totally spent on wage-goods. Thus, it is clear that the total gross profit is again equal to the sum of capitalists' consumption and investment. The equation:

$$P = C_c + I$$

holds good also for an economy with commodity taxes.

Let us now examine what will happen if the rate of taxation on wage-goods is increased, say from 3 to 5 per cent, and the proceeds of the tax spent on behalf of the unemployed.

According to our assumptions made in the preceding para-graph, the rate of investment I and the capitalist's propensity to consume will not change immediately upon the introduction of such increased taxes. Hence, the gross profit $P = C_c + I$ and employment will remain at the old level as at the beginning of the new taxation régime. If, however, employment, and thus the wage bill, has not changed, while the sum of doles has increased by the amount of the new tax revenue, it is clear that the total demand for wage-goods has also risen by 2 per cent. But so has also the marginal cost of wage-goods, and in this situation it is obvious that the prices of wage-goods will be increased also by 2 per cent, while their output has remained unchanged; in this way a new short-period equilibrium is established which differs from the former one only in that the wage-goods' marginal costs and prices both are increased by 2 per cent.† No stimulus exists in this new situation for the change of capitalists' consumption or investment. Thus if the spending of capitalists does not change immediately after the increase of taxation, neither does it change later; nor does gross profit change, since it is equal to the capitalists' spending.

It must be added, however, that this is true only under an additional assumption. For though the volume and structure of output have not changed, the nominal value of output has increased. Thus demand for cash is greater, and the rate of interest tends to rise, exerting a depressing influence on investment. We shall assume here that this increase is very small, i.e. that the supply of cash for transactions is elastic.

It is easy to see from the above that the change in distribution of national income caused by the increase of wage-goods taxation consists chiefly in the shift of purchasing power from workers and officials to the dole receivers. Real wages and State officials' salaries fall in the case considered by 2 per cent, while the 'real' capitalists' consumption is a much smaller proportion, since only a certain not very great percentage of their expenditure is devoted to wage-goods.

3. We shall now go a step farther, and introduce into our system taxes on capitalists' incomes. For the sake of simplicity, we suppose that the rate of taxation is a constant percentage. It is obvious that these taxes are not prime costs, but form a part of gross profits. The entrepreneurs continue to maximise the difference between sales and prime costs, e.g. wages, cost of raw materials, commodity taxes, etc.; for the greater this differential, the greater the income from the enterprise remaining after the payment of income tax.

† This is not quite precise. The capitalists' consumption is partly directed to wage-goods, the increase in the price of which may cause a rise of capitalists' expenditure on wage-goods and a fall in the purchases of other goods subject to their consumption. Then a corresponding shift in the output will take place.

National income can be represented in the same way as before:

Gross profits	Capitalists' consumption
Wages	Investment
Commodity taxes	Consumption of wage-goods

But now the consumption of wage-goods is covered not only by wages and commodity taxes, but also by income taxes. It is evident that gross profit P is now equal to the sum of capitalists' consumption C_c, investment I, and income-tax revenue T_i:

$$P = (C_c + I) + T_i$$

and the part of P received by capitalists is equal to $C_c + I$.

Next we shall consider what happens if the income tax is raised, again for the purpose of dole payments, say from 15 to 25 per cent. According to our assumptions no change of investment and capitalists' consumption will happen in the period immediately succeeding the introduction of the additional tax. Thus, the immediate result of an increased income tax is a rise of gross profit $P = (C_c + I) + T_i$ because of the rise of T_i; employment is pushed to a point at which the gross profit is greater by the amount of the increment of T_i. This is not at all surprising, for new State expenditure has taken place, while at no other point was the spending curtailed. But conceivably such is not the final effect, because of the influence of the income tax on the profitability of investment.

It is clear that the income tax must raise the rate of interest, otherwise the net reward for lending would be diminished. If, for instance, the rate of interest is initially at 3 per cent, the reward for lending with a 15 per cent income tax will be 2·55 per cent; likewise it is clear that with the increase of income tax to 25 per cent the rate of interest rises to 3·4 per cent (3·4 per cent reduced by 25 per cent gives 2·55 per cent).

Now, if the prospective rate of profit of a certain type of investment is initially at 9 per cent, let us say, and the rate of interest at 3 per cent, the entrepreneur planning investment has a differential of 6 per cent before income tax deduction and

39

5·1 per cent after the deduction of 15 per cent income tax to cover his risk. But at the new level of taxation the rate of interest is 3·4 per cent, and only 5·6 per cent remains as net profit and income tax; further, because of the increase of the income tax, we have now to deduct 25 per cent from that difference, leaving 4·2 per cent for net profit, while before the introduction of the increased tax there was a 5·1 per cent differential. The difference of 0·9 per cent is equal to the charge of 'new' 25 per cent − 15 per cent = 10 per cent income tax on the 9 per cent prospective rate of profit. There is nothing surprising in this fact, since the lenders' reward is not diminished by an increase in the income tax, and therefore the whole burden falls on the entrepreneur planning investment. In this way this whole burden exerts pressure on the inducement to invest.

It would be premature to conclude that *this* is the final result. One must take into account that in the first period of the new taxation régime the gross profit increased by just the amount of the total 'new taxes'. Thus if the entrepreneurs expected the future returns to increase by the same amount as the present ones have done, which seems probable (for instance the prospective rate of profit of 9 per cent by 0·9), this would be just enough to counterbalance the depressive influence of income tax on the inducement to invest.

Thus total income of capitalists $(C_c + I)$ remains unaltered. Consequently, the gross profit $P = (C_c + I) + T_i$ in which the component T_i has risen, is likely to increase, as is employment also. (We are assuming that the supply of cash for transactions is elastic.)

In this way the chief change resulting from income taxation would be the rise of the demand for wage-goods on the part of the unemployed. This raises, of course, not only the output of wage-goods, but also their prices, and thus reduces the 'real' consumption of workers employed before the introduction of the new tax. On the other hand, there will be an increase in consumption on the part of new employed workers. What rise in total real wage-bill results, depends, of course, on the elasticity of supply of wage-goods.

4. In the last stage of our argument we introduce capital taxation. We may, for example, imagine a tax to be levied on every type of owned capital at the rate of 2 per cent per year. Of course, as with income taxation, it does not constitute a prime cost. Thus, with the help of an argument similar to that applied in the last paragraph, we obtain for the gross profit, the equation:

$$P = (C_c + I) + T_i + T_c$$

where T_i is the total amount of income taxes and T_c that of capital taxes.

Let us examine the effect of raising the rate of capital tax, the proceeds of which continue to be used for dole payments. Again according to our assumptions the investment I and the capitalists' consumption C_c remain unaltered immediately after the introduction of the new tax. Thus the first effect of the latter is such an increase of employment that the gross profits P rise by the amount of the increment of T_c.

Here, however, the course of events does not follow the same path as in the case of income taxation. It is not difficult to see that the increase of the rate of capital taxation does not tend to lower the net profitability of investment (which covers the risk) or to raise the rate of interest. Indeed, if somebody borrows money and builds a factory, he does not increase his own capital by this action and does not pay a greater capital tax. And if he ventures his own means, he also pays the same tax as he would if he abstained from investment. Thus the net profitability of investment is unaffected by capital taxation. Unlike income tax, the capital tax is not a cost of production in the long run either.

In the same way, everybody is ready to lend at the current rate of interest; for whether he lends money or not does not affect the capital tax he pays.

Thus we see that the inducement to invest is not weakened by an increase of the rate of capital tax if the expected returns were the same as before. But because the gross profit

$$P = (C_c + I) + T_i + T_c$$

has increased under the new taxation régime these expectations are improved. The inducement to invest is now stronger than before the introduction of the additional taxes. Investment consequently increases and causes a new rise of gross profit P and of employment.

Curiously enough, capital taxation not only makes the gross profit rise by the total amount of this taxation, but also the income $C_c + I$, which remains to capitalists after they have paid the taxes, increases significantly. (In the case of income taxation $C_c + I$ remains unaltered and the gross profit is increased by the amount of the taxation.)

The increase via the real wage-bill is higher than in the case of income taxation, due to the stronger rise of employment.

It follows from the above that capital taxation is perhaps the best way to stimulate business and reduce unemployment. It has all the merits of financing the State expenditure by borrowing, but is distinguished from borrowing by the advantage of the State not becoming indebted. It is difficult to believe, however, that capital taxation will ever be applied for this purpose on a large scale; for it may seem to undermine the principle of private property, and therefore in this case, as in general, 'any government which had both the power and the will to remedy the major defects of the capitalist system would have the will and the power to abolish it altogether'.[†]

[†] Joan Robinson, Review of R. F. Harrod, 'The Trade Cycle', *Economic Journal*, December 1936.

PART II

5. COSTS AND PRICES

[(1943) 1954]

'COST-DETERMINED' AND 'DEMAND-DETERMINED' PRICES

Short-term price changes may be classified into two broad groups; those determined mainly by changes in cost of production and those determined mainly by changes in demand. Generally speaking, changes in the prices of finished goods are 'cost-determined' while changes in the prices of raw materials inclusive of primary foodstuffs are 'demand-determined'. The prices of finished goods are affected, of course, by any 'demand-determined' changes in the prices of raw materials but it is through the channel of *costs* that this influence is transmitted.

It is clear that these two types of price formation arise out of different conditions of supply. The production of finished goods is elastic as a result of existing reserves of productive capacity. When demand increases it is met mainly by an increase in the volume of production while prices tend to remain stable. The price changes which do occur result mainly from changes in costs of production.

The situation with respect to raw materials is different. The increase in the supply of agricultural products requires a relatively considerable time. This is true, although not to the same extent, with respect to mining. With supply inelastic in short periods, an increase in demand causes a diminution of stocks and a consequent increase in price. This initial price movement may be enhanced by the addition of a speculative element. The commodities in question are normally standardized and are

43

subject to quotation at commodity exchanges. A primary rise in demand which causes an increase in prices is frequently accompanied by secondary speculative demand. This makes it even more difficult in the short run for production to catch up with demand.

The present chapter will be devoted mainly to the study of the formation of 'cost-determined' prices.

PRICE FIXING BY A FIRM

Let us consider a firm with a given capital equipment. It is assumed that supply is elastic, i.e. that the firm operates below the point of practical capacity and that the prime costs (cost of materials and wages†) per unit of output are stable over the relevant range of output.‡ In view of the uncertainties faced in the process of price fixing it will not be assumed that the firm attempts to maximize its profits in any precise sort of manner. Nevertheless, it will be assumed that the actual level of over-heads does not directly influence the determination of price since the total of overhead costs remains roughly stable as output varies. Thus, the level of output and prices at which the sum of overheads and profits may be supposed to be highest is at the same time the level which may be considered to be most favour-able to profits. (It will be seen at a later stage, however, that the level for overheads may have an indirect influence upon price formation.)

In fixing the price the firm takes into consideration its average prime costs and the prices of other firms producing similar products. The firm must make sure that the price does not become too high in relation to prices of other firms, for this

---

† Salaries are included in overheads.

‡ In fact unit prime costs fall somewhat in many instances as output increases. We abstract from this complication which is of no major importance.

The assumption of an almost horizontal short-run prime cost curve was made in my *Essays on the Theory of Economic Fluctuations*, back in 1939. Since that time it has been proved by many empirical inquiries and has played explicitly or implicitly an important role in economic research. (Cf., for instance, W. W. Leontief: *The Structure of American Economy*, 1941, Harvard University Press.)

would drastically reduce sales, and that the price does not become too low in relation to its average prime cost, for this would drastically reduce the profit margin. Thus, when the price p is determined by the firm in relation to unit prime cost u, care is taken that the ratio of p to the weighted average price of all firms, $\bar{p}$† does not become too high. If u increases, p can be increased proportionately only if $\bar{p}$ rises proportionately as well. But if $\bar{p}$ increases less than u, the firm's price p will also be raised less than u. These conditions are clearly satisfied by the formula

$$p = mu + n\bar{p} \qquad (5.1)$$

where both m and n are positive coefficients.

We postulate that $n < 1$ and this for the following reason. In the case where the price p of the firm considered is equal to the average price $\bar{p}$ we have:

$$p = mu + np$$

from which it follows that n must be less than one.

The coefficients m and n characterizing the price-fixing policy of the firm reflect what may be called the degree of monopoly of the firm's position. Indeed, it is clear that equation (5.1) describes semi-monopolistic price formation. Elasticity of supply and stability of unit prime costs over the relevant range of output is incompatible with so-called perfect competition. For, if perfect competition were to prevail the excess of the price p over the unit prime costs u would drive the firm to expand its output up to the point where full capacity is reached. Thus, any firm remaining in the business would work up to capacity, and the price would be pushed up to the level which equilibrates demand and supply.

For the analysis of changes in the degree of monopoly it is convenient to use diagrammatic presentation. Let us divide equation (5.1) by the unit prime cost u:

$$\frac{p}{u} = m + n\frac{\bar{p}}{u}$$

† Weighted by the respective outputs and inclusive of the firm in question.

45

This equation is represented in Fig. 5.1, where $\bar{p}/u$ is taken as abscissa and p/u as ordinate, by a straight line AB. The inclination of AB is less than $45°$ because $n < 1$. The position of this straight line which is fully determined by m and n reflects the degree of monopoly. When, as a result of change in m and n, the straight line moves up from the position of AB to that of

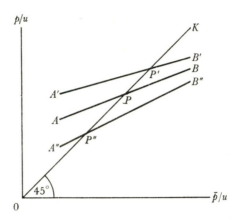

FIG. 5.1. Changes in the degree of monopoly.

$A'B'$, then to a given average price $\bar{p}$ and unit prime cost u there corresponds a higher price p of the firm over the relevant range of $\bar{p}/u$. We shall say in this case that the degree of monopoly increases. When, on the other hand, the straight line moves down to the position $A''B''$ we shall say that the degree of monopoly diminishes. (We assume that m and n always change in such a way that none of the lines corresponding to various positions of AB intersect each other over the relevant range of $\bar{p}/u$.)

We may now demonstrate a proposition which is of some importance to our future argument. Let us take into consideration the points of intersection P, P', P'' of the straight lines AB, $A'B'$, $A''B''$ with the like OK drawn through zero point at $45°$. It is clear that the higher the degree of monopoly the larger the abscissa of the respective point of intersection. Now this point is determined by the equations:

$$\frac{p}{u} = m + n\frac{\bar{p}}{u} \quad \text{and} \quad \frac{p}{u} = \frac{\bar{p}}{u}$$

It follows that the abscissa of the point of intersection is equal to $m/(1-n)$. Consequently a higher degree of monopoly will be reflected in the increase of $m/(1-n)$ and conversely.

In this section and the subsequent one the discussion of the influence of the degree of monopoly upon price formation is rather formal in character. The actual reasons for the changes in the degree of monopoly are examined at a later stage.

PRICE FORMATION IN AN INDUSTRY: A SPECIAL CASE

We may commence the discussion of the determination of average price in an industry by considering a case where the coefficients m and n are the same for all firms, but where their unit prime costs u differ. We have then on the basis of equation (5.1):

$$p_1 = mu_1 + n\bar{p}$$
$$p_2 = mu_2 + n\bar{p} \qquad (5.1')$$
$$\cdots\cdots\cdots$$
$$p_k = mu_k + n\bar{p}$$

If these equations are weighted by their respective outputs (that is, multiplied each by its respective output, all added and the sum divided by the aggregate output) we obtain:

$$\bar{p} = m\bar{u} + n\bar{p}$$

so that
$$\bar{p} = \frac{m}{1-n}\bar{u} \qquad (5.2)$$

Let us recall that according to the preceding section the higher the degree of monopoly the higher is $m/(1-n)$. We thus can conclude: The average price $\bar{p}$ is proportionate to the average unit prime cost $\bar{u}$ if the degree of monopoly is given. If the degree of monopoly increases, $\bar{p}$ rises in relation to $\bar{u}$.

It is still important to see in what way a new 'price equilibrium' is reached when the unit prime costs change as a result of changes in prices of raw materials or unit wage costs. Let us denote the 'new' unit prime costs by u_1, u_2, etc., and the 'old' prices by p_1', p_2', etc. The weighted average of these prices is $\bar{p}'$. To this correspond new prices p_1'', p_2'', etc., equal to $mu_1 + n\bar{p}'$, $mu_2 + n\bar{p}'$, etc. This leads in turn to a new average price, $\bar{p}''$, and so on, the process finally converging to a new value of $\bar{p}$ given by formula (5.2). This convergence of the process depends on the condition $n < 1$. Indeed, from equations (5.1') we have:

$$\bar{p}'' = m\bar{u} + n\bar{p}'$$

and for the new final $\bar{p}$:

$$\bar{p} = m\bar{u} + n\bar{p}$$

Subtracting the latter equation from the former we obtain:

$$\bar{p}'' = \bar{p} = n\,(\bar{p}' - \bar{p})$$

which shows that the deviation from the final value $\bar{p}$ diminishes in geometric progression, given $n < 1$.

PRICE FORMATION IN AN INDUSTRY:
GENERAL CASE

We shall now consider the general case where the coefficients m and n differ from firm to firm. It appears that by a procedure similar to that applied in the special case the formula

$$\bar{p} = \frac{\bar{m}}{1 - \bar{n}}\,\bar{u} \qquad (5.2')$$

is reached. $\bar{m}$ and $\bar{n}$ are weighted averages of the coefficients m and n.†

Let us now imagine a firm for which the coefficients m and n

† $\bar{m}$ is the average of m weighted by total prime costs of each firm; $\bar{n}$ is the average of n weighted by respective outputs.

are equal to $\bar{m}$ and $\bar{n}$ for the industry. We may call it a representative firm. We may further say that the degree of monopoly of the industry is that of the representative firm. Thus, the degree of monopoly will be determined by the position of the straight line corresponding to

$$\frac{p}{u} = \bar{m} + \bar{n}\frac{\bar{p}}{u}$$

A rise in the degree of monopoly will be reflected in the upward shift of this straight line (see Fig. 5.1). It follows from the argument on p. 47 that the higher the degree of monopoly, according to this definition, the higher is $\bar{m}/(1 - \bar{n})$.

From this and from equation (5.2′) there follows the generalization of the results obtained in the preceding section for a special case. The average price p is proportionate to the average unit prime cost $\bar{u}$ if the degree of monopoly is given. If the degree of monopoly increases, p rises in relation to $\bar{u}$.

The ratio of average price to average prime cost is equal to the ratio of the aggregate proceeds of industry to aggregate prime costs of industry. It follows that the ratio of proceeds to prime costs is stable, increases or diminishes depending on what happens to the degree of monopoly.

It should be recalled that all of the results obtained here are subject to the assumption of elastic supply. When firms reach their practical capacity a further rise in demand will cause a price increase beyond the level indicated by the above considerations. However, this level might be maintained for some time while the firm allows orders to pile up.

CAUSES OF CHANGE IN THE
DEGREE OF MONOPOLY

We shall confine ourselves herein to a discussion of the major factors underlying changes in the degree of monopoly in modern capitalist economies. First and foremost the process of concentration in industry leading to the formation of giant corporations should be considered. The influence of the emergence of firms representing a substantial share of the output of an industry can be readily understood in the light of the above considerations. Such a firm knows that its price p influences appreciably the average price $\bar{p}$ and that, moreover, the other firms will be pushed in the same direction because their price formation depends on the average price $\bar{p}$. Thus, the firm can fix its price at a level higher than would otherwise be the case. The same game is played by other big firms and thus the degree of monopoly increases substantially. This state of affairs can be reinforced by tacit agreement. (Such an agreement may take *inter alia* the form of price fixing by one large firm, the 'leader', while other firms follow suit.) Tacit agreement, in turn, may develop into a more or less formal cartel agreement which is equivalent to full scale monopoly restrained merely by fear of new entrants.

The second major influence is the development of sales promotion through advertising, selling agents, etc. Thus, price competition is replaced by competition in advertising campaigns, etc. These practices also will obviously cause a rise in the degree of monopoly.

In addition to the above, two other factors must be considered: (*a*) the influence of changes in the level of overheads in relation to prime costs upon the degree of monopoly, and (*b*) the significance of the power of trade unions.

If the level of overheads should rise considerably in relation to prime costs, there will necessarily follow a 'squeeze of profits' unless the ratio of proceeds to prime costs is permitted to rise. As a result, there may arise a tacit agreement among the firms of an industry to 'protect' profits, and consequently to increase prices in relation to unit prime costs. For instance, the increase in capital costs per unit of output as a result of the introduction of techniques which increase capital intensity may tend to raise the degree of monopoly in this way.

The factor of 'protection' of profits is especially apt to appear during periods of depression. The situation in such periods is as follows. Aggregate proceeds would fall in the same proportion as prime costs if the degree of monopoly remained unchanged. At the same time aggregate overheads by their very nature fall in depression less than prime costs. This provides a background for tacit agreements not to reduce prices in the same proportion as prime costs. As a result there is a tendency for the degree of monopoly to rise in the slump, a tendency which is reversed in the boom.†

Although the above considerations show a channel through which overheads may affect price formation, it is clear that their influence upon prices in our theory is much less clear-cut than that of prime costs. The degree of a monopoly *may*, but need not necessarily, increase as a result of a rise in overheads in relation to prime costs. This and the emphasis on the influence of prices of other firms constitute the difference between the theory presented here and the so-called full cost theory.

Let us turn now to the problem of the influence of trade-union strength upon the degree of monopoly. The existence of powerful trade unions may tend to reduce profit margins for the following reasons. A high ratio of profits to wages strengthens the bargaining position of trade unions in their demands for wage increases since higher wages are then compatible with 'reasonable profits' at existing price levels. If after such increases are granted prices should be raised, this would call forth new demands for wage increases. It follows that a high ratio of profits to wages cannot be maintained without creating a tendency towards rising costs. This adverse effect upon the competitive position of a firm or an industry encourages the adoption of a policy of lower profit margins. Thus, the degree of monopoly will be kept down to some extent by the activity of trade unions, and this the more the stronger the trade unions are.

The changes in the degree of monopoly are not only of decisive importance for the distribution of income between workers and capitalists, but in some instances for the distribu-

---

† This is the basic tendency; however, in some instances the opposite process of cut-throat competition may develop in a depression.

tion of income within the capitalist class as well. Thus, the rise in the degree of monopoly caused by the growth of big corporations results in a relative shift of income to industries dominated by such corporations from other industries. In this way income is redistributed from small to big business.

THE LONG-RUN AND SHORT-RUN COST–PRICE RELATIONS

The cost–price relations arrived at above were based on short-run considerations. However, the only parameters which enter the equations in question are the coefficients m and n reflecting the degree of monopoly. These may, but need not necessarily, change in the long run. If m and n *are* constant, the long-run changes in prices will reflect only the long-run changes in unit prime costs. Technological progress will tend to reduce the unit prime cost u. But the *relations* between prices and unit prime costs can be affected by changes in equipment and technique only to the extent to which they influence the degree of monopoly.† The latter possibility was indicated above when it was mentioned that the degree of monopoly may be influenced by the level of overheads in relation to prime costs.

It should be noticed that the whole approach is in contradiction to generally accepted views. It is usually assumed that as a result of increasing intensity of capital, i.e. increasing amount of fixed capital per unit of output, there is of necessity a continuous increase in the ratio of price to unit prime cost. The view is apparently based on the assumption that the sum of overheads and profits varies in the long run roughly proportionately with the value of capital. Thus, the rise in capital in relation to output is translated into a higher ratio of overheads plus profits to proceeds, and the latter is equivalent to an increase in the ratio of prices to unit prime costs.

---

† This, however, is qualified by the assumption underlying our cost–price equations, namely that the unit prime cost does not depend on the degree of utilization of equipment and that the limit of practical capacity is not reached. See p. 44.

Now, it appears that profits plus overheads may show a long-run fall in relation to the value of capital and as a result the ratio of price to unit prime cost may remain constant even though capital increases in relation to output. This is illustrated by developments in American manufacturing in the period from 1899 to 1914. (See Table 5.1.)

TABLE 5.1 *Capital intensity and the ratio of proceeds to prime costs in manufacturing in the United States, 1899–1914*

| Year | Ratio of real fixed capital to production | Ratio of overheads and profits | | Ratio of proceeds to prime costs |
| | | To book value of fixed capital | To value of fixed capital at current prices | |
	1899 = 100			(%)
1899	100	100	100	133
1904	111	95	96	133
1909	125	89	84	133
1914	131	80	73	132

SOURCE: National Bureau of Economic Research; Paul H. Douglas, *The Theory of Wages*; United States Census of Manufactures. For details see Statistical Appendix, Note 1.

As will be seen from the table, fixed capital rose continuously in relation to production over the period considered, while the ratio of proceeds to prime costs remained roughly stable. This is explained by a fall in profits plus overheads in relation to the value of fixed capital (both in relation to its book value and in relation to its value at current prices).

There remains, of course, the possibility stated above that the rise in overheads in relation to prime costs as a result of the increase in capital intensity may cause a rise in the degree of monopoly because of a tendency to 'protect' profits; this tendency, however, is by no means automatic and may not materialize, as is shown by the above example.

We have dealt above with certain questions which arise in connection with the application of our theory to the long-run phenomena. When this theory is applied to the analysis of price formation in the course of a business cycle, the problem arises whether our formulae hold good in the boom. Indeed, in such periods the utilization of equipment may reach the point of practical capacity and thus, under the pressure of demand, prices may exceed the level indicated by these formulae. It seems, however, that as a result of the availability of reserve capacities and the possibility of increasing the volume of equipment whenever bottlenecks occur, this phenomenon is not frequently encountered even in booms. In general, it seems to be restricted to war or post-war developments, where shortages of raw materials or equipment limit severely the supply in relation to demand. It is this type of increase in prices which is the basic reason for the inflationary developments prevailing in such periods.

APPLICATION TO THE LONG-RUN CHANGES IN UNITED STATES MANUFACTURING

As the ratio of price to unit prime cost is equal to the ratio of aggregate proceeds to aggregate prime costs, the changes in this ratio can be analysed empirically for various industries on the basis of the United States Census of Manufactures which gives the value of products, the cost of materials and the wage bill for each industry. However, the changes in the ratio of proceeds to prime costs for a single industry which, according to the above, are determined by changes in the degree of monopoly, reflect changes in conditions particular to that industry. For instance, a change in the price policy of one big firm may cause a fundamental change in the degree of monopoly in that industry. For this reason we limit our considerations here to the manufacturing industry as a whole, and thus are able to interpret the changes in the ratio of proceeds to prime cost in terms of major changes in industrial conditions.

We thus take into consideration the ratio of the aggregate proceeds of United States manufacturing to its aggregate prime

costs. The following difficulty, however, arises. This ratio does not reflect merely the changes in the ratios of proceeds to prime costs of single industries, but also shifts in their importance in manufacturing as a whole. For this reason, in Table 5.2 is given not only the ratio of proceeds to prime costs of United States manufacturing, but also such a ratio calculated on the assumption that from one period to another the relative share of major industrial groups in the aggregate value of proceeds is stable.†
The actual difference between these two series appears to be in general not significant.

TABLE 5.2 *Ratio of proceeds to prime costs in manufacturing in the United States, 1879–1937*

Year	Original data (%)	Assuming stable industrial composition, base year 1899 (%)
1879	122·5	124·0
1889	131·7	131·0
1899	133·3	133·3
1914	131·6	131·4
1923	133·0	132·7
1929	139·4	139·6
1937	136·3	136·8

SOURCE: United States Census of Manufactures.

It will be seen that there is a substantial increase in the ratio of proceeds to prime costs from 1879 to 1889. It is generally known that this period marked a change in American capitalism characterized by the formation of giant industrial corporations. It is thus not surprising that the degree of monopoly increased in that period.

From 1889 to 1923 there is little change in the ratio of pro-

† The details of the calculation, as well as the adjustments which have been made in order to assure approximate comparability for various census years which was upset by the changes in the scope and methods of the Census, are described in the Statistical Appendix, Notes 2 and 3.

ceeds to prime costs. A marked increase, however, appears again in the period 1923–29. The rise in the degree of monopoly in this period is partly accounted for by what may be called a 'commercial revolution'—a rapid introduction of sales promotion through advertising, selling agents, etc. Another factor was a general increase in overheads in relation to prime costs which occurred in this period.

It may be questioned whether the high level of the ratio of proceeds to prime costs in 1929 was not due, at least partly, to firms reaching their full capacity in the boom. It should be noticed, however, that the degree of utilization of equipment was not higher in 1929 than in 1923. It also appears from the consideration of the Census figures in 1925 and 1927 that the rise in ratio of proceeds to prime costs in the period 1923–9 was gradual in character.

From 1929 to 1937 the ratio of proceeds to prime costs shows a moderate reduction. This can probably be attributed largely to the rise in the power of trade unions.

The explanations given here are tentative and sketchy in character. Indeed, the interpretation of the movement of the ratio of proceeds to prime cost in terms of changes in the degree of monopoly is really the task of the economic historian who can contribute to such a study a more thorough knowledge of changing industrial conditions.

APPLICATION TO UNITED STATES MANUFACTURING
AND RETAIL TRADE DURING THE GREAT DEPRESSION

In Table 5.3 the ratio of proceeds to prime costs for United States manufacturing is given for 1929, 1931, 1933, 1935 and 1937. Again, in addition to the original ratio of proceeds to prime cost the ratio adjusted for changes in composition in the value of products is given.† As in the previous table, the two series do not differ significantly. For this period the ratio of

† As in the preceding table, the figures were adjusted for changes in the scope and methods of the Census (see Statistical Appendix, Notes 2 and 3).

Costs and prices

aggregate retail sales of consumption goods in the United States to their cost to retailers is also available. This corresponds roughly to the ratio of proceeds to prime costs for the retail trade and is included in Table 5.3 (a series adjusted for composition of sales was not calculated).

TABLE 5.3 *Ratio of proceeds to prime costs in manufacturing and retail trade in the United States, 1929–37*

	Ratio of proceeds to prime costs in manufacturing industries		Ratio of sales to costs in retail trade
Year	Original data	Assuming stable industrial composition base year 1929 (%)	
1929	139·4	139·4	142·0
1931	143·3	142·2	144·7
1933	142·8	142·3	148·8
1935	136·6	136·7	140·8
1937	136·6	136·6	140·7

SOURCE: United States Census of Manufactures; B. M. Fowler and W. H. Shaw, 'Distributive Costs of Consumption Goods', *Survey of Current Business*, July 1942.

It will be seen that the ratio of proceeds to prime costs tended to increase in the depression; but taking into consideration the extent of the depression in the 'thirties the change is very moderate. The increase in the ratio can be attributed to a rise in overheads in relation to prime costs, which fostered tacit agreements to 'protect' profits and thus to raise the degree of monopoly. It will be seen that during the recovery from 1933 to 1937 there was a reverse movement. For manufacturing, however, the ratio of proceeds to prime cost fell to a level which was significantly lower than in 1929. As suggested in the preceding section, this is probably the result of a considerable strengthening of trade unions in the period 1933–7.

57

FLUCTUATIONS IN PRICES OF RAW MATERIALS

As stated at the beginning of this chapter, short-run changes in the prices of primary products largely reflect changes in demand. Thus they fall considerably during downswings and rise substantially during upswings.

It is known that prices of raw materials undergo larger cyclical fluctuations than wage rates. The causes of this phenomenon can be explained as follows. Even with constant wage rates the prices of raw materials would fall in a depression as a result of a slump in 'real' demand. Now, the cuts in money wages during a depression can never 'catch up' with the price of raw materials because wage cuts in turn cause a fall in demand and hence a new fall in the prices of primary products. Imagine that the prices of raw materials fall by 20 per cent as a result of the slump in real demand. Imagine further that the wage rate is cut subsequently by 20 per cent also. The theory of price formation developed above shows that the general price level will in consequence also fall by around 20 per cent. (The degree of monopoly is likely to increase somewhat but not much.) But this will cause a corresponding fall in incomes, demand, and thus in prices of raw materials.

In Table 5.4 below, indices of prices of raw materials and hourly earnings in the United States in the period 1929–41 are compared.

The ratio of prices of raw materials to hourly wages shows a long-run downward trend which in part reflects the rise in productivity of labour. This, however, does not obscure the cyclical pattern which is manifested in particular in the decided fall in both the slump of 1929–33 and that of 1937–8.

PRICE FORMATION OF FINISHED GOODS

The formation of prices of finished goods according to the above theory is the result of price formation at each stage of production on the basis of the formula:

$$\bar{p} = \frac{\bar{m}}{1 - \bar{n}} \bar{u} \tag{5.2}$$

Costs and prices

TABLE 5.4. *Indices of prices of raw materials and of hourly earnings in manufacturing, mining, construction and railroads in the United States, 1929–41*

Year	Prices of raw materials	Hourly earnings	Ratio of prices of raw materials to hourly earnings
1929	100·0	100·0	100·0
1930	86·5	99·1	87·3
1931	67·3	94·5	71·2
1932	56·5	82·1	68·8
1933	57·9	80·9	71·6
1934	70·4	93·8	75·1
1935	79·1	98·0	80·7
1936	81·9	99·5	82·3
1937	87·0	109·6	79·4
1938	73·8	111·1	66·4
1939	72·0	112·3	64·1
1940	73·7	115·7	63·7
1941	85·6	126·6	67·6

SOURCE: Department of Commerce, *Statistical Abstract of the United States, Survey of Current Business, Supplement.*

With a given degree of monopoly, prices at each stage are proportionate to unit prime costs. In the first stage of production, prime costs consist of wages and the cost of primary products. In the next stage the prices are formed on the basis of the prices of the previous stage and the wages of the present stage, and so on. It is easy to see, therefore, that, with a given degree of monopoly, prices of finished goods are homogeneous linear functions of prices of primary materials on the one hand, and of wage costs at all stages of production on the other.

Since fluctuations of wages in the course of the business cycle are much smaller than those of prices of raw materials (see the preceding section) it follows directly that prices of finished goods also tend to fluctuate considerably less than prices of raw materials.

As to different categories of prices of finished goods, it has been frequently assumed that the prices of investment goods during a depression fall more than prices of consumption goods. There is no basis for such a contention in the present theory. There may even be a certain presumption in favour of some fall in the prices of consumption goods in relation to the prices of investment goods. The weight of primary products inclusive of food is probably higher in the aggregate in the case of consumption goods than in the case of investment goods and the prices of primary products fall during a depression more than wages.

In Table 5.5 are given the indices of prices of raw materials, of consumer prices (at retail level) and of prices of finished investment goods for the United States in the period 1929–41. It will be seen that the prices of raw materials showed much larger fluctuations than the prices of finished consumption or investment goods.

TABLE 5.5 *Indices of prices of raw materials, consumption goods and investment goods in the United States, 1929–41*

Year	Prices of raw materials	Prices of consumption goods†	Prices of investment goods†	Ratio of prices of investment goods to prices of consumption goods
1929	100·0	100·0	100·0	100·0
1930	86·5	95·3	97·2	102·0
1931	67·3	85·3	89·2	104·3
1932	56·5	75·0	80·3	107·1
1933	57·9	71·5	78·3	109·5
1934	70·4	75·8	85·8	113·2
1935	79·1	77·8	84·7	108·9
1936	81·9	78·5	87·3	111·2
1937	87·0	81·5	92·4	113·4
1938	73·8	79·6	95·8	120·4
1939	72·0	78·9	94·4	119·6
1940	73·7	79·8	96·9	121·4
1941	85·6	84·8	102·9	121·3

SOURCE: Department of Commerce, *Survey of Current Business*.

† Price indices implicit in the deflation of consumption and fixed capital investment calculated from *National Income Supplement to Survey of Current Business*, 1951. It is clear that these indices are of Paasche type.

Costs and prices

The ratio of the prices of investment goods to the prices of consumption goods shows a distinct rising trend. However, from the time-curve of this ratio in Fig. 5.2 it is apparent that there was a more pronounced rise during the downswings of 1929–33 and 1937–8† than in the period considered as a whole. It appears on the other hand that these cyclical fluctuations of the ratio of the prices of investment goods to the prices of consumption goods although clearly marked are rather small in amplitude.

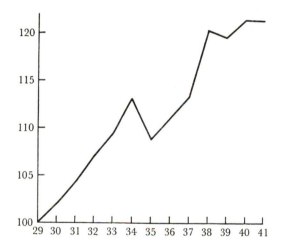

FIG. 5.2. Ratio of prices of investment goods to prices of consumption goods, United States, 1929–41.

† In the latter case, however, the phenomenon seems to have been exaggerated by special factors.

6. DISTRIBUTION OF
NATIONAL INCOME

[(1938) 1954]

We shall now link the ratio of proceeds to prime costs in an industry, which we discussed in the previous chapter, with the relative share of wages in the value added of that industry. The value added, i.e. the value of products less the cost of materials, is equal to the sum of wages, overheads and profits. If we denote aggregate wages by W, the aggregate cost of materials by M, and the ratio of aggregate proceeds to aggregate prime cost by k, we have:

$$\text{overheads} + \text{profits} = (k-1)(W+M)$$

where the ratio of proceeds to prime costs k is determined, according to the above, by the degree of monopoly. The relative share of wages in the value added of an industry may be represented as

$$w = \frac{W}{W+(k-1)(W+M)}$$

If we denote the ratio of the aggregate cost of materials to the wage bill by j, we have:

$$w = \frac{1}{1+(k-1)(j+1)} \qquad (6.1)$$

It follows that the relative share of wages in the value added is determined by the degree of monopoly and by the ratio of the materials bill to the wage bill.

A similar formula to that established for a single industry can now be written for the manufacturing industry as a whole.

However, here the ratio of proceeds to prime costs and the ratio of the cost of materials to wages depend also on the importance of particular industries in manufacturing taken as a whole. In order to separate this element we can proceed as follows. In formula (6.1), for k, the ratio of proceeds to prime costs, and for j, the ratio of the materials bill to the wage bill, we substitute the ratios k' and j', adjusted in such a way as to eliminate the effect of changes in the importance of particular industries. Thus we obtain:

$$w' = \frac{1}{1 + (k'-1)(j'+1)} \tag{6.1'}$$

The relative share of wages in the value added, w', obtained in this way will deviate from the actual relative share of wages, w, by an amount which will be due to changes in the industrial composition of value added.

Of the parameters in formula (6.1') k' is determined by the degree of monopoly in manufacturing industries. The problem of determinants of j' is somewhat more complicated. Prices of materials are determined by the prices of primary products, by wage costs at the lower stages of production and by the degree of monopoly at those stages. Thus, roughly speaking, j', which equals the ratio of unit costs of materials to unit wage costs, is determined by the ratio of prices of primary products to unit wage costs and by the degree of monopoly in manufacturing.†
To summarize: the relative share of wages in the value added of manufacturing is determined, apart from the industrial composition of the value added, by the degree of monopoly and by the ratio of raw material prices to unit wage costs. A rise in the degree of monopoly or in raw material prices in relation to unit wage costs causes a fall of the relative share of wages in the value added.

It should be recalled in this connection that as distinguished

† This rough generalization is based on two simplifying assumptions: (*a*) that unit costs of materials change proportionately with prices of materials, i.e. changing efficiency in the utilization of materials is not taken into account; and (*b*) that unit wage costs at the lower stages of production vary proportionately with unit wage costs at higher stages.

from prices of finished goods the prices of raw materials are 'demand determined'. The ratio of raw material prices to unit wage costs depends on the demand for raw materials, as determined by the level of economic activity, in relation to their supply which is inelastic in the short run (cf. pp. 43 and 58).

We can now consider in much the same way as above a group of industries broader than manufacturing where the pattern of price formation may be assumed to be similar, namely manufacturing, construction, transportation and services. For this group as a whole the relative share of wages in the aggregate value added will decrease with an increase in the degree of monopoly or an increase in the ratio of prices of primary products to unit wage costs. The result will also be affected, of course, by changes in the industrial composition of the value added of the group.

It may now be shown that this theorem can be generalized to cover the relative share of wages in the gross national income of the private sector (i.e. national income gross of depreciation exclusive of income of government employees). In addition to the sectors of the economy accounted for above, we have still to consider agriculture and mining, communications and public utilities, trade, real estate and finance. In agriculture and mining the products are raw materials and the relative share of wages in the value added depends mainly on the ratio of prices of the raw materials *produced* to their unit wage costs. In the remaining sectors the relative share of wages in the value added is negligible. It will thus be seen that, broadly speaking, the degree of monopoly, the ratio of prices of raw materials to unit wage costs and industrial composition† are the determinants of the relative share of wages in the gross income of the private sector.

† It should be noticed that by industrial composition we mean the composition of the *value* of the gross income of the private sector. Thus, changes in the composition depend not only on changes in the *volume* of the industrial components but also on the relative movement of the respective prices.

Distribution of national income

The long-run changes in the relative share of wages, whether in the value added of an industrial group such as manufacturing or in the gross income of all the private sector, are, according to the above, determined by long-run trends in the degree of monopoly, in the prices of raw materials in relation to unit wage costs, and in industrial composition. The degree of monopoly has a general tendency to increase in the long run and thus to depress the relative share of wages in income, although, as we have seen above, this tendency is much stronger in some periods than in others. It is difficult, however, to generalize about the relation of raw material prices to unit wage costs (which depends on long-run changes in the demand–supply position of raw materials) or about industrial composition. No *a priori* statement is therefore possible as to the long-run trend of the relative share of wages in income. As we shall see in the next section, the relative share of wages in the value added of United States manufacturing declined considerably after 1880, whereas in the United Kingdom wages maintained their share in the national income from the 'eighties to 1924, showing long-run ups and downs in the intervening period.

It is possible to say something more specific about changes in the relative share of wages in income in the course of the business cycle. We have found that the degree of monopoly is likely to increase somewhat during depressions (cf. p. 51). Prices of raw materials fall in the slump in relation to wages (cf. p. 58). The former influence tends to reduce the relative share of wages in income and the latter to increase it. Finally, changes in industrial composition during a depression affect the relative share of wages adversely. Indeed, these changes are dominated by a reduction of investment in relation to other activities and the relative share of wages in the income of investment goods industries is generally higher than in other industries. (In communications, public utilities, trade, real estate and finance, particularly, wage payments are relatively unimportant.)

The net effect of changes in these three factors upon the relative share of wages in income—of which the first and the third are negative and the second positive—appears to be small. Thus, the relative share of wages, whether in the value added of an industrial group or in the gross income of the private sector as a whole, does not seem to show marked cyclical fluctuations.

The above may be illustrated: (*a*) by an analysis of the long-run changes in the relative share of wages in the value added of United States manufacturing and in the national income of the United Kingdom; (*b*) by an analysis of changes in the relative share of wages in the value added of United States manufacturing during the Great Depression; and (*c*) by an analysis of changes during the same period in the relative share of wages in the national income of the United States and the United Kingdom.

LONG-RUN CHANGES IN THE RELATIVE SHARE OF WAGES IN THE VALUE ADDED OF UNITED STATES MANUFACTURING AND IN THE NATIONAL INCOME OF THE UNITED KINGDOM

The long-run changes in the relative share of wages in the value added of United States manufacturing are analysed in Table 6.1. In the first two columns k' and j' are given, i.e. the 'adjusted' ratio of proceeds to prime costs and the 'adjusted' ratio of the materials bill to the wage bill.† From these two series w', the adjusted relative share of wages in the value added, is derived by employing formula (6.1′). Finally, the actual relative share of wages in the value added is given. The changes in the difference $w-w'$ indicate the influence of changes in the industrial composition of value added.

† The 'adjusted' ratio of proceeds to prime costs, k', is the same series as in Table 5.3 above. For the original values of the ratio of the materials bill to the wage bill and for the description of the calculation of the 'adjusted' series j' given in Table 6.1, see Statistical Appendix, Notes 2 and 3. The adjustments introduced for changes in the scope and methods of the Census are also described there.

TABLE 6.1 *Relative share of wages in value added in manufacturing in the United States, 1879–1937*

Year	Ratio of proceeds to prime costs (%) k'	Ratio of materials bill to wage bill (%) j'	Share of wages in value added (%) w'	Share of wages in value added (%) w
	Assuming stable industrial composition (base year 1899)			Original data
1879	124·0	355	47·8	47·8
1889	131·0	297	44·8	44·6
1899	133·3	337	40·7	40·7
1914	131·4	341	41·9	40·2
1923	132·7	292	43·8	41·3
1929	139·6	311	38·1	36·2
1937	136·3	298	40·9	38·6

SOURCE: United States Census of Manufactures.

It appears that w, the actual relative share of wages in the value added, suffered a considerable though not quite continuous fall over the period considered. This fall resulted mainly from the increase in the 'adjusted' ratio of proceeds to prime costs, k', which in our interpretation reflects a rise in the degree of monopoly. The 'adjusted' ratio of the materials bill to the wage bill, j', tended to fall rather than to rise and thus in general its changes mitigated the decline in w. Finally, the effect of changes in industrial composition was to reduce the actual relative share of wages in the value added w: indeed, the latter fell more than its adjusted value w'.

No data exist with respect to the relative share of wages in the national income of the United States over a long period. Such data, however, are available for the United Kingdom.

In Table 6.2, the relative share of wages in the national home-produced income† of the United Kingdom is given. The table

† Home-produced national income is national income exclusive of income from foreign investments, which is irrelevant to the problem of distribution considered here. It should be noticed that even after this adjustment the data do not correspond fully to our concepts because they relate to net rather than to gross national

includes in addition the ratio of the Sauerbeck index of whole-sale prices to the index of wage rates which can be taken as an approximate indicator of changes in the ratio of prices of raw materials to unit wage costs. Although the Sauerbeck index is a general index of wholesale prices, it is based mainly on prices of raw materials and semi-manufactures. It is true that the

TABLE 6.2. *Relative share of wages in the home-produced national income of the United Kingdom, 1881–1924*

Period	Relative share of wages (%)	Ratio of Sauerbeck index of wholesale prices to index of wage rates (1881 = 100)
1881–1885	40·0	93·6
1886–1890	40·5	80·8
1891–1895	41·7	73·5
1896–1900	40·7	70·6
1901–1905	39·8	72·4
1906–1910	37·9	78·3
1911–1913	37·1	82·1
1924	40·6	69·6

SOURCE: A. R. Prest, 'National Income of the United Kingdom', *Economic Journal*, March 1948; Unpublished estimates of U.K. income from overseas by F. Hilgerdt; *Statist*; A. L. Bowley, 'Wages and Income in the United Kingdom Since 1860', Table 1, p. 6, Woods' index of wage rates.

index of wage rates rises more quickly (or falls more slowly) than the index of wage costs, due to the secular increase in productivity, and thus a decreasing trend is involved in our indicator of the ratio of raw material prices to unit wage costs. However, this trend is likely to be slow, especially since the wage-rate index is partly based on piece rates. It is therefore very likely that the ratio of prices of raw materials to wage costs fell from 1881–5 to 1891–5 as did the indicator. It certainly rose from 1896–1900 to 1911–13; and it fell again from 1911–13 to 1924.

income and because national income includes the income of government employees while we dealt above with the relative share of wages in the income of the private sector. However, it seems probable that these factors could not affect seriously the trend of the relative share of wages in the national income.

Distribution of national income

The movement of the relative share of labour in the national income may be plausibly interpreted in the following way. While there was a long-run rise in the degree of monopoly, its influence was largely offset by the fall in the ratio of raw material prices to unit wage costs from 1881–5 to 1891–5. The influence of the degree of monopoly was reinforced by the rise of the ratio of raw material prices to unit wage costs in the period 1896–1900 to 1911–13, and finally more than offset by a fall in this ratio from 1911–13 to 1924. Thus, the fact that the relative share of wages in the national income was about the same in 1924 as in 1881–5, would be, according to this interpretation, the result of the accidental balancing of the influence of changes in the degree of monopoly and changes in the ratio of raw material prices to unit wage costs. Unfortunately, this interpretation cannot be considered conclusive because of the possible influence of changes in the industrial composition of national income.

CHANGES IN THE RELATIVE SHARE OF WAGES IN THE VALUE ADDED OF UNITED STATES MANUFACTURING DURING THE GREAT DEPRESSION

In Table 6.3, changes in the relative share of wages in the value added of United States manufacturing during the Great Depression are analysed by employing the same method as that used for the analysis of long-run changes. (Cf. Table 6.1.) The table contains the 'adjusted' ratio of proceeds to prime costs k', and the 'adjusted' ratio of the material bill to the wage bill j'.

From k' and j' is calculated w'—the 'adjusted' relative share of wages in the value added—by means of formula (6.1'). Finally, the actual relative share of wages in the value added, w, is given. The changes in the difference $w-w'$ reflect the effect of changes in industrial composition.

If we abstract tentatively from the influence of changes in industrial composition, and thus take into consideration only k', j' and w', the following picture emerges. From 1929 to 1933

69

Dynamics of capitalist economy

TABLE 6.3 *Relative share of wages in value added in manufacturing in the United States, 1929–37*

Year	Ratio of proceeds to prime costs (%) Assuming stable industrial composition (base year 1929) k'	Ratio of materials bill to wage bill (%) j'	Share of wages in value added (%) w'	Share of wages in value added (%) Original data w
1929	139·4	346	36·2	36·2
1931	142·2	307	36·8	35·7
1933	142·3	312	36·4	35·0
1935	136·7	314	39·7	37·9
1937	136·6	331	38·8	38·6

SOURCE: United States Census of Manufactures. For details see Statistical Appendix, Notes 2 and 3, below.

the ratio of proceeds to prime costs, k', increases, reflecting the rise in the degree of monopoly during a depression (cf. p. 57). However, at the same time, the ratio of the materials bill to the wage bill declines as a result of the fall, typical for a slump, in the prices of raw materials in relation to wages. The influence of these two factors upon the relative share of wages in the value added, w', is in opposite directions. As w' was stable from 1929 to 1933 it appears that these two factors were in balance. From 1933 to 1937 the 'adjusted' relative share of the wages in the value added, w', increased as a result of the fall in the 'adjusted' ratio of proceeds to prime costs, k', which was not offset by the rise in the 'adjusted' ratio of the materials bill to the wage bill, j'. This situation reflects the relatively great reduction in the degree of monopoly in the recovery resulting from the increased power of trade unions. The long-run tendency for prices of raw materials to fall relative to wage costs, which is reflected in the fact that j' did not recover in 1937 to its 1929 level, was a contributory factor.

As to the difference between the actual and 'adjusted' relative share of wages in the value added, w–w', it appears that it fell in the depression (w fell somewhat from 1929 to 1933, while w' remained roughly stable; from 1933 to 1937 w increased a little more than w'.) This is mainly due to the greater decline in production of investment goods than in total manufacturing production during the slump. Indeed, the relative share of wages in the value added is higher for these goods than for manufactured goods as a whole and thus the reduction in the importance of the output of investment goods during a depression tends to reduce the relative share of wages in the value added of manufacturing as a whole.

It is of some interest to establish the weight of the three factors considered above in determining the movement of the relative share of wages in the value added during the course of the cycle. For this purpose we may calculate from the formula (6.1′) what the value of w' would be in 1933 if only the ratio of proceeds to prime costs changed while the ratio of the materials bill to the wage bill remained at its 1929 level. The result is 34·6 per cent. This figure, together with the value of w in 1929 and 1933 and the value of w' in 1933 (cf. Table 6.3), enables us to construct Table 6.4.

TABLE 6.4. *Analysis of changes in the relative share of wages in value added in manufacturing in the United States from 1929 to 1933*

Item	Relevant years			
Proceeds ÷ prime costs	1929	1933	1933	1933
Materials bill ÷ wage bill	1929	1929	1933	1933
Industrial composition	1929	1929	1929	1933
Relative share of wages in value added	36·2	34·6	36·4	35·0
Difference		−1·6	+1·8	−1·4

The difference between the second and the first columns gives the effect of the change in the ratio of proceeds to prime costs; that between the third and second columns the effect of the change in the ratio of the materials bill to the wage bill; and that between the fourth and the third columns the effect of the change in the industrial composition.

It will be seen that the effects of the three factors considered are relatively small. Thus, their balance is also small and this accounts for the approximate stability of the relative share of wages in the value added during the depression.

CHANGES IN THE RELATIVE SHARE OF WAGES IN THE NATIONAL INCOME IN THE UNITED STATES AND THE UNITED KINGDOM DURING THE GREAT DEPRESSION

Unfortunately, no exact data exist on this subject for the United States because national income statistics do not give wages separately from salaries. It is possible, however, to form an approximate idea about changes in the relative share of wages in the gross income of the private sector for the period 1929–37. The data on wages in manufacturing industries are available.†

As mentioned above, wage payments are negligible in some industrial groups, namely in trade (shop assistants being classified as salary earners), finance and real estate, communications and public utilities. For the remaining industries, namely agriculture, mining, construction, transport, and services, only salaries and wages combined are available. If we now calculate a weighted index of wages in manufacturing on the one hand and of salaries and wages in agriculture, mining, construction, transport, and services on the other, we obtain an approximation to the index of the total wage bill. (Indeed, wages in manufacturing constitute about half of total wages, while salaries in the remaining industries under consideration move to some extent parallel with wages.) We further divide this index by that of the gross income of the private sector and in this way obtain an approximate index of the relative share of wages in this income (Table 6.5).

† The series of payrolls is available for all years; it agrees with the Census of Manufactures for the Census years.

Distribution of national income

TABLE 6.5. *Approximation to the index of relative share of wages in gross income of the private sector in the United States, 1929–37*

Year	Index of wages in manufacturing	Index of wages and salaries in agriculture, mining, construction, transport and services	Combined index
	In relation to gross income of the private sector		
1929	100·0	100·0	100·0
1930	94·1	105·3	99·7
1931	90·8	109·5	100·1
1932	87·6	113·9	100·8
1933	100·2	109·3	104·8
1934	107·8	102·7	105·3
1935	106·7	96·2	101·5
1936	110·8	99·3	105·1
1937	116·4	96·7	106·6

SOURCE: United States Census of Manufactures, Department of Commerce, *National Income Supplement to Survey of Current Business, 1951*. For details see Statistical Appendix, Note 4, below.

This series shows a slow upward long-run trend which can be attributed mainly to a fall in the degree of monopoly as a result of the strengthening of trade unions after 1933 and to some extent to a decline in prices of raw materials in relation to wage costs. The cyclical fluctuations are obviously small. (If salaries in agriculture, mining, construction, transportation, and services were eliminated, the index would be somewhat lower during the depression because salaries in general fall somewhat less than wages; but there is no doubt that the cyclical fluctuations would remain small.) This result is most likely due to the interaction of the same factors which emerged from the analysis of the relative share of wages in the value added of manufacturing industries.

During the depression there was probably a rise in the degree of monopoly in the 'wage-paying' industries, but a fall in the prices of raw materials in relation to wages. The changes in the industrial composition of the private sector during the slump tended to reduce the relative share of wages. Indeed, there was a relative shift in the distribution of national income from 'wage-paying' industries to other industries; and also within the 'wage-paying' group from industries with a higher relative share to those with a lower relative share of wages in gross income. These shifts were due mainly to the relatively greater reduction during the depression of investment activity. Thus, as in the manufacturing industries, the adverse effect of the rise in the degree of monopoly and of the change in industrial composition upon the relative share of wages in the gross income during the depression, appears to have been roughly offset by the influence of the fall of prices of raw materials in relation to wages.

We may now consider the relation between wages and home-produced national income in the United Kingdom in the period 1929–38.† There are available two national income series for the period in question; one estimated by Professor A. L. Bowley and the other by Mr J. R. S. Stone. However, there exists only the Bowley estimate of the wage bill. Fortunately, however, the indices of both variants of national income are in general very similar in the period in question although their absolute values differ.

In Table 6.6 are given the indices of the ratios of the wage bill (as estimated by Bowley) to the two variants of national income. It will be seen that both series display no marked cyclical fluctuations.

CYCLICAL CHANGES IN THE RELATIVE SHARE OF WAGES AND SALARIES IN THE GROSS INCOME OF THE PRIVATE SECTOR

We have dealt above only with changes in the relative share of wages in aggregate income. We shall now consider briefly the

† As mentioned above (see footnote to p. 67), the United Kingdom series of home-produced national income does not correspond exactly to the concept of gross income of the private sector used by us since the national income is net of depreciation and includes salaries of government officials. It appears, however, that in the period considered the changes in the relative share of wages in the national income thus defined are indicative of the changes corresponding to our concept.

TABLE 6.6. *Indices of relative share of wages in national income in the United Kingdom, 1929–1938*

Year	Wage bill (Bowley) in relation to national income (Bowley)	Wage bill (Bowley) in relation to national income (Stone)
1929	100·0	100·0
1930	97·6	100·0
1931	98·4	98·8
1932	99·8	99·1
1933	95·3	96·8
1934	96·9	98·5
1935	96·8	98·0
1936	96·7	97·5
1937	102·4	97·9
1938	98·1	97·4

SOURCE: A. L. Bowley, Studies in the National Income; A. R. Prest, 'National Income of the United Kingdom', *Economic Journal*, March 1948; *Board of Trade Journal*.

problem of the relative share of labour as a whole in the gross income of the private sector by taking into account not only wages but salaries as well. The application of the theory of income distribution to the analysis of long-run changes in the relative share of wages and salaries in income would be difficult because of the growing importance of salaries in the sum of overheads and profits as a result of increasing concentration of business. However, cyclical fluctuations in the relative share of wages and salaries in the gross income of the private sector can be examined and are of considerable interest.

We have seen above that the relative share of wages in the gross income of the private sector tends to be fairly stable in the course of the cycle. This cannot be expected, however, for the relative share of wages and salaries combined. Salaries, because of their 'overhead' character, are likely to fall less during the depression and to rise less during the boom than wages. Thus the 'real' wage and salary bill, V, can be expected to fluctuate less during the course of the cycle than the 'real' gross income of the private sector, Y.† Consequently, we can write:

$$V = \alpha Y + B$$

where B is a positive constant in the short period although subject to long-run changes. The coefficient α is less than 1 because $V < Y$ and $B > 0$. If we now divide both sides of this equation by the 'real' income Y we obtain

$$\frac{V}{Y} = \alpha + \frac{B}{Y} \tag{6.2}$$

where V/Y is the relative share of wages and salaries in the gross income of the private sector. V/Y increases, of course, when the 'real' income Y declines. It may be noticed here that equation (6.2) constitutes one link in the theory of the business cycle developed below.

We now shall apply equation (6.2) to the United States data for the period 1929–41. The relative share of wages and salaries‡ in the gross income of the private sector and the value of this income at 1939 prices are given in Table 6.7.§ In accordance with equation (2) we correlate the relative share of wages and salaries in income V/Y with the reciprocal of 'real' income $1/Y$ and also with time t to allow for possible secular trend. (t is counted in years from 1935, which is the middle point of the period.) We obtain the following regression equation:

$$\frac{V}{Y} 100 = 42 \cdot 5 + \frac{707}{Y} + 0 \cdot 11 t$$

The double correlation coefficient is 0·926. The value of V/Y calculated from the regression equation is given in Table 6.7 as well. The positive trend probably reflects the influence of the fall in the degree of monopoly and in the prices of raw materials in relation to unit wage costs.

† We imagine both the wage and salary bill and the gross income of the private sector to be deflated by the same price index.

‡ It should be noticed that in salaries are included those of higher business executives which are rather akin to profits.

§ As a deflator, the index implicit in the deflation of the real gross product of the private sector by the United States Department of Commerce was used. For details see Statistical Appendix, Notes 5 and 6.

Distribution of national income

TABLE 6.7. *Relative share of wages and salaries in gross income of the private sector in the United States, 1929–41*

Year	Relative share of wages and salaries in gross income of the private sector $(V/Y) . 100$ (%)	Gross income of the private sector at 1939 prices Y ($ billion)	Calculated relative share of wages and salaries in gross income of the private sector (%)
1929	50·0	74·1	51·0
1930	52·4	65·9	52·6
1931	55·0	59·3	54·1
1932	57·9	48·0	57·0
1933	57·8	46·9	57·1
1934	56·0	51·9	55·8
1935	52·7	57·7	54·5
1936	53·4	65·5	53·2
1937	53·3	69·0	52·6
1938	53·2	64·3	54·2
1939	53·5	68·8	53·6
1940	52·1	75·9	52·3
1941	51·4	89·6	51·0

SOURCE: United States Department of Commerce, *National Income Supplement to Survey of Current Business, 1951*.

7. THE DETERMINANTS OF PROFITS

[(1933) 1954]

We may consider first the determinants of profits in a closed economy in which both government expenditure and taxation are negligible. Gross national product will thus be equal to the sum of gross investment (in fixed capital and inventories) and consumption. The value of gross national product will be divided between workers and capitalists, virtually nothing being paid in taxes. The income of workers consists of wages and salaries. The income of capitalists or gross profits includes depreciation and undistributed profits, dividends and withdrawals from unincorporated business, rent and interest. We thus have the following balance sheet of the gross national product, in which we distinguish between capitalists' consumption and workers' consumption:

Gross profits	Gross investment
Wages and salaries	Capitalists' consumption
	Workers' consumption
Gross national product	*Gross national product*

If we make the additional assumption that workers do not save, then the workers' consumption is equal to their income. It follows directly then:

Gross profits = Gross investment + capitalists' consumption

What is the significance of this equation? Does it mean that profits in a given period determine capitalists' consumption and investment, or the reverse of this? The answer to this question depends on which of these items is directly subject to the decisions of capitalists. Now, it is clear that capitalists may

78

decide to consume and to invest more in a given period than in the preceding one, but they cannot decide to earn more. It is, therefore, their investment and consumption decisions which determine profits, and not vice versa.

If the period which we consider is short, we may say that the capitalists' investment and consumption are determined by decisions shaped in the *past*. For the execution of investment orders takes a certain time, and capitalists' consumption responds to changes in the factors which influence it only with a certain delay.

If capitalists always decided to consume and to invest in a given period what they had earned in the preceding period, the profits in the given period would be equal to those in the preceding one. In such a case profits would remain stationary, and the problem of interpreting the above equation would lose its importance. But such is *not* the case. Although profits in the preceding period are one of the important determinants of capitalists' consumption and investment, capitalists in general do *not* decide to consume and invest in a given period precisely what they have earned in the preceding one. This explains why profits are *not* stationary, but fluctuate in time.

The above argument requires certain qualifications. Past investment decisions may not fully determine the volume of investment in a given period, owing to unexpected accumulation or running down of stocks. The importance of this factor, however, seems to have been frequently exaggerated.

A second qualification arises out of the fact that consumption and investment decisions will usually be made in real terms, and in the meantime prices may change. For instance, a piece of ordered capital equipment may now cost more than at the time when the order was given. To get over this difficulty both sides of the equation will be assumed to be calculated at constant prices.

We may now conclude that the real gross profits in a given short period are determined by decisions of capitalists with respect to their consumption and investment shaped in the past, subject to correction for unexpected changes in the volume of stocks.

For the understanding of the problems considered it is useful to present the above from a somewhat different angle. Imagine that following the Marxian 'schemes of reproduction' we sub-divide all the economy into three departments: department I producing investment goods, department II producing consumption goods for capitalists, and department III producing consumption goods for workers. The capitalists in department III, after having sold to workers the amount of consumption goods corresponding to their wages, will still have left a surplus of consumption goods which will be the equivalent of their profits. These goods will be sold to the workers of department I and department II, and as the workers do not save it will be equal to their incomes. Thus, total profits will be equal to the sum of profits in department I, profits in department II, and wages in these two departments: or, total profits will be equal to the value of production of these two departments—in other words, to the value of production of investment goods and consumption goods for capitalists.

The production of department I and department II will also determine the production of department III if the distribution between profits and wages in all departments is given. The production of department III will be pushed up to the point where profits earned out of that production will be equal to the wages of departments I and II. Or, to put it differently, em-ployment and production of department III will be pushed up to the point where the surplus of this production over what the workers of this department buy with their wages is equal to the wages of departments I and II.

The above clarifies the role of the 'distribution factors', i.e. factors determining the distribution of income (such as degree of monopoly) in the theory of profits. Given that profits are determined by capitalists' consumption and investment, it is the workers' income (equal here to workers' consumption) which is determined by the 'distribution factors'. In this way capitalists' consumption and investment conjointly with the 'distribution factors' determine the workers' consumption and consequently the national output and employment. The national output will be pushed up to the point where profits carved out of it in accordance with the 'distribution factors' are equal to the sum of capitalists' consumption and investment.†

THE GENERAL CASE

We may now pass from our simplified model to the real situation where the economy is not a closed system and where government expenditure and taxation are not negligible. The gross national product is then equal to the sum of gross investment, consumption, government expenditure on goods and services, and the surplus of exports over imports. ('Investment' here stands for private investment, public investment being included in government expenditure on goods and services.) Since the total value of production is divided between capitalists and workers or paid in taxes, the value of gross national product on the income side will be equal to gross profits net of taxes, wages and salaries net of taxes, plus all taxes direct and indirect. We thus have the following balance sheet of the gross national product:

Gross profits net of (direct) taxes	Gross investment
	Export surplus
Wages and salaries net of (direct) taxes	Government expenditure on goods and services
Taxes (direct and indirect)	Capitalists' consumption
	Workers' consumption
Gross national product	*Gross national product*

Part of the taxes are spent on transfers such as social benefits, while the remaining part serves to finance government expen-

---

† The above argument is based on the assumption of elastic supply which was made in Part I. However, if the output of consumption goods for workers is at capacity level any increase in capitalists' consumption or investment will merely cause a rise in prices of these goods. In such a case it is the rise in prices of consumption goods for workers which will increase profits in department III up to a point where they are equal to the higher amount of wages in departments I and II. Real wage rates will fall, reflecting the fact that an increased wage bill meets an unchanged supply of consumption goods.

diture on goods and services. Let us subtract from both sides of the balance sheet, taxes minus transfers. On the income side the item 'Taxes' will disappear and we shall add transfers to wages and salaries. On the other side, the difference between government expenditure on goods and services and taxes minus transfers will be equal to the budget deficit. Thus, the balance sheet will be as follows:

Gross profits
   net of taxes
Wages, salaries and
   transfers net of taxes
	Gross investment
	Export surplus
	Budget deficit
	Capitalists' consumption
	Workers' consumption

Gross national products
   minus taxes plus transfers
	Gross national product
	   minus taxes plus transfers

By subtracting now from both sides wages, salaries and transfers net of taxes, we obtain the following equation:

$$\text{Gross profits net of taxes} = \begin{cases} \text{Gross investment} \\ + \text{Export surplus} \\ + \text{Budget deficit} \\ - \text{Workers' saving} \\ + \text{Capitalists' consumption} \end{cases}$$

Thus, this equation differs from the equation of the simplified model in that instead of investment we have now investment plus export surplus plus budget deficit minus workers' saving. It is clear, however, that our previous relationship still obtains if we assume that both the budget and foreign trade are balanced and that the workers do not save, that is:

$$\text{Gross profits after tax} = \text{Gross investment} + \text{capitalists' consumption}$$

Even if these assumptions are made, the system is much more realistic than in the first simplified model and all of the arguments of the previous section still apply. It has to be remembered, however, that we are dealing now with profits after tax, while in the first simplified model the problem did not arise because taxes were assumed to be negligible.

Determinants of profits

Let us subtract on both sides of the general equation for profits (see previous page) capitalists' consumption and add workers' savings. We obtain:

Capitalists' gross savings	Gross investment
Workers' savings	Export surplus
	Budget deficit
Total gross savings	*Total gross savings*

Thus, total savings are equal to the sum of private investment, export surplus and budget deficit, while capitalists' savings are, of course, equal to this sum minus workers' savings.

If we now assume that both foreign trade and the government budget are balanced we obtain:

$$\text{Gross savings} = \text{Gross investment}$$

If we assume, moreover, that workers do not save we have:

$$\text{Capitalists' gross savings} = \text{Gross investment}$$

This equation is equivalent to:

$$\text{Gross profits} = \text{Gross investment} + \text{Capitalists' consumption}$$

because it may be obtained from the latter equation by the deduction of capitalists' consumption from both sides.

It should be emphasized that the equality between savings and investment plus export surplus plus budget deficit in the general case—or investment alone in the special case—will be valid under all circumstances. In particular, it will be independent of the level of the rate of interest which was customarily considered in economic theory to be the factor equilibrating the demand for and supply of new capital. In the present conception investment, once carried out, automatically provides the savings necessary to finance it. Indeed, in our simplified model, profits in a given period are the direct outcome of capitalists' consumption and investment in that period. If investment increases by a certain amount, savings out of profits are *pro tanto* higher.

6-2

To put it in a more concrete fashion: if some capitalists increase their investment by using for this purpose their liquid reserves, the profits of other capitalists will rise *pro tanto* and thus the liquid reserves invested will pass into the possession of the latter. If additional investment is financed by bank credit, the spending of the amounts in question will cause equal amounts of saved profits to accumulate as bank deposits. The investing capitalists will thus find it possible to float bonds to the same extent and thus to repay the bank credits.

One important consequence of the above is that the rate of interest cannot be determined by the demand for and supply of new capital because investment 'finances itself'. The factors determining the level of the rate of interest are discussed in Part III below.

THE EFFECT OF THE EXPORT SURPLUS
AND BUDGET DEFICIT

In what follows we shall frequently assume a balanced government budget and balanced foreign trade, as well as zero workers' savings, which will enable us to base our argument on the equality between profits after taxes and the sum of gross investment and capitalists' consumption. It is useful, however, to say a few words now about the significance of the influence of the export surplus and the budget deficit on profits.

According to the formula established above, profits are equal to investment plus export surplus plus budget deficit minus workers' savings plus capitalists' consumption. It follows directly that an increase in the export surplus will raise profits *pro tanto* if other components are unchanged. The mechanism involved is the same as that described on p. 80. The value of an increment in the production of the export sector will be accounted for by the increase in profits and wages of that sector. The wages, however, will be spent on consumption goods. Thus, production of consumption goods for workers will be expanded up to the point where profits out of this production will increase by the amount of additional wages in the export sector.†

It follows directly from the above that the export surplus enables profits to increase above that level which would be determined by capitalists' investment and consumption. It is from this point of view that the fight for foreign markets may be viewed. The capitalists of a country which manages to capture foreign markets from other countries are able to increase their profits at the expense of the capitalists of the other countries. Similarly, a colonial metropolis may achieve an export surplus through investment in its dependencies.‡

A budget deficit has an effect similar to that of an export surplus. It also permits profits to increase above the level determined by private investment and capitalists' consumption. In a sense the budget deficit can be considered as an artificial export surplus. In the case of the export surplus a country receives more for its exports than it pays for its imports. In the case of the budget deficit the private sector of the economy receives more from government expenditure than it pays in taxes. The counterpart of the export surplus is an increase in the indebtedness of the foreign countries towards the country considered. The counterpart of the budget deficit is an increase in the indebtedness of the government towards the private sector. Both of these surpluses of receipts over payments generate profits in the same way.

The above shows clearly the significance of 'external' markets (including those created by budget deficits) for a capitalist

† If the production of consumption goods for workers is at capacity level, prices of these goods will rise up to a point where profits out of this production will increase by the amount of additional wages in the export sector (cf. footnote to p. 81)

‡ Foreign lending by a given country need not be associated with exports of goods from that country. If a country *A* lends to country *B*, the latter can spend the proceeds of the loan in country *C*, which may increase *pro tanto* its stock of gold and liquid foreign assets. In this case foreign lending by country *A* will cause an export surplus in country *C* accompanied by an accumulation of gold or liquid foreign assets in that country. In the case of colonial dependencies, this situation is not apt to arise, i.e. the amount invested will be normally spent in the metropolis.

economy. Without such markets profits are conditioned by the ability of capitalists to consume or to undertake capital investment. It is the export surplus and the budget deficit which enable the capitalists to make profits over and above their own purchases of goods and services.

The connection between 'external' profits and imperialism is obvious. The fight for the division of existing foreign markets and the expansion of colonial empires, which provide new opportunities for export of capital associated with export of goods, can be viewed as a drive for export surplus, the classical source of 'external' profits. Armaments and wars, usually financed by budget deficits, are also a source of this kind of profits.

PROFITS AND INVESTMENT UNDER SIMPLIFYING ASSUMPTIONS

It was noted above (p. 79) that capitalists' investment and consumption are determined by decisions shaped in the *past*. The determinants of investment decisions, which are rather complex in character, are considered in Chapter 10 below. We shall deal here with the determination of capitalists' consumption.

We may make the following assumption, which is plausible as a first approximation, about the 'real' capitalists' consumption in a given year, C_t: that it consists of a stable part A and a part proportionate to $P_{t-\lambda}$, the real profits after tax of some time ago; that is:

$$C_t = qP_{t-\lambda} + A \tag{7.1}$$

where λ indicates the delay of the reaction of capitalists' consumption to the change in their current income. q is positive and < 1 because capitalists tend to consume only a part of the increment in income. In fact, this part is likely to be rather small so that q is probably considerably less than 1. Finally, A is a constant in the short run although subject to long-run changes. We shall assume for the time being that foreign trade and the government budget are balanced and that workers do not save. In this case profits after tax P are equal to the sum of investment I and capitalists' consumption C:

$$P = I + C \qquad (7.2)$$

Substituting the value of C from equation (5) we obtain:

$$P_t = I_t + qP_{t-\lambda} + A \qquad (7.3)$$

It follows that 'real' profits at time t are determined by current investment and profits at the time $t-\lambda$. Profits at the time $t-\lambda$ will be in turn determined by investment at that time and by profits at the time $t-2\lambda$, and so on. It is thus clear that profits at time t are a linear function of investment at time t, $t-\lambda$, $t-2\lambda$, etc., and that the coefficients of investment I_t, $I_{t-\lambda}$, $I_{t-2\lambda}$, etc., in this relation will be 1, q, q^2, etc., respectively. Now q, as said above, is less than 1 and probably considerably less than 1. Thus the series of coefficients 1, q, q^2,...will be quickly decreasing and consequently among I_t, $I_{t-\lambda}$, $I_{t-2\lambda}$,... only those relatively near in time will count in the determination of profits, P_t. Profits will thus be a function both of current investment and of investment in the near past; or, roughly speaking, profits follow investment with a time lag. We can thus write as an approximate equation:

$$P_t = f(I_{t-\omega}) \qquad (7.4)$$

where ω is the time lag involved.

The shape of the function f can be determined as follows. Let us go back for a moment to equation (7.3) and substitute for P its value from equation (7.4):

$$f(I_{t-\omega}) = I_t + qf(I_{t-\omega-\lambda}) + A$$

This equation should be fulfilled whatever the course in time of investment I_t. Thus, it should cover *inter alia* the case where investment is maintained for some time at a stable level so that we have $I_t = I_{t-\omega} = I_{t-\omega-\lambda}$. It follows:

$$f(I_t) = I_t + qf(I_t) + A$$

or

$$f(I_t) = \frac{I_t + A}{1 - q}$$

87

Dynamics of capitalist economy

As this equality is fulfilled for any level of I_t, it gives us the shape of the function f. We thus can write the equation (7.4) as:

$$P_t = \frac{I_{t-\omega} + A}{1 - q} \qquad (7.4')$$

The significance of equation $(7.4')$ is in that it reduces the number of determinants of profits from two to one as a result of taking into consideration the dependence of capitalists' consumption on past profits as given by equation (7.1). Profits according to equation $(7.4')$ are determined fully by investment with a certain time lag being involved. Moreover, investment depends on investment decisions still farther back in time. It follows that profits are determined by past investment decisions.

The interpretation of equation $(7.4')$ may give rise to certain difficulties. Under the given assumptions that foreign trade and the government budget are balanced and that workers do not save, investment is equal to capitalists' savings (see p. 83). It thus follows directly from equation $(7.4')$ that capitalists' savings 'lead' profits. This result may appear paradoxical. 'Common sense' would suggest the opposite sequence—namely, that savings are determined by profits. This, however, is not the case. Capitalists' consumption in a certain period is the result of their decisions based on past profits. Since profits usually change in the meantime, actual savings do *not* correspond to the intended disposition of income. Indeed, actual savings which are equal to investment *will* 'lead' profits as shown by equation $(7.4')$. How this happens may be illustrated by the following example. Imagine that for some time both investment and thus savings and also profits are constant. Imagine that there is a sudden increase in investment. Savings will increase immediately together with investment, and profits will rise by the same amount. However, capitalists' consumption will rise only after some time as a result of this primary increase in profits. Thus, profits will still be increasing after the rise in investment and savings has already come to a stop.

Determinants of profits

How will equation (7.4') change if we do *not* postulate that foreign trade and the government budget are balanced and that workers' savings are zero? If we denote the sum of private investment, export surplus and budget deficit by I', workers' savings by s and capitalists' consumption as above by C, we have for profits the equation (see p. 83):

$$P = I' - s + C$$

It will be seen that for this general case equation (8') will be modified to:

$$P_t = \frac{I'_{t-\omega} - s_{t-\omega} + A}{1 - q} \qquad (7.4'')$$

Indeed, the formula (7.4') was obtained from the relation between capitalists' consumption and profits (equation 7.1)and from the assumption that investment I is equal to the difference between profits and capitalists' consumption. Thus, when this difference is equal to $I' - s$, it is this item that should replace I in formula (7.4').

Equation (7.4'') may be replaced by a simpler although approximate formula. It should be remembered that total savings are equal to the sum of investment, export surplus and budget deficit, I' (see p. 83). Further, although in general workers' savings, s, are not equal to zero, their level and absolute changes are small as compared with total savings. Moreover, s must show in the course of the business cycle a pronounced correlation with total savings. (This follows from our considerations in the next chapter which establish a relation between profits and national income.) Thus, $I' - s$ must be closely correlated with I'. We have consequently as a good approximation:

$$P_t = \frac{I'_{t-\omega} + A'}{1 - q'} \qquad (7.4''')$$

where the change of parameters from q to q' and from A to A' reflects the replacement of $I'_{t-\omega} - s_{t-\omega}$ by a linear function of

$I'_{t-\omega}$. It should be remembered that q is a coefficient indicating what part of an increment in profit will be devoted to consumption while the constant A is that part of capitalists' consumption which is stable in the short-run although subject to long-run changes. q' and A' reflect in addition the relation of workers' savings to total savings which are equal to I'.

The formula $(7.4''')$ is superior to formula $(7.4'')$ in that it may be illustrated statistically. This is virtually impossible for $(7.4'')$ because no statistical data about workers' savings, s, are available.

STATISTICAL ILLUSTRATION

We shall apply equation $(7.4''')$ to the United States data for the period 1929–40. The 'real' values of gross profits after tax, $P\dagger$ and of I' are given in Table 7.1. The meaning of I' is slightly

TABLE 7.1 *Determination of profits in the United States, 1929–40*

Year	Gross profits after taxes P_t	Gross private investment plus export surplus plus budget deficit plus brokerage fees I'_t	$I'_{t-\frac{1}{2}}$	Calculated gross profits after taxes
		(Billions of dollars at 1939 prices)		
1929	33·7	14·2	13·7	33·2
1930	28·5	10·2	11·2	29·6
1931	24·5	5·5	6·7	23·3
1932	18·3	3·2	3·8	19·2
1933	17·6	3·4	3·3	18·2
1934	20·4	6·0	5·3	20·6
1935	24·4	8·4	7·8	23·7
1936	26·8	11·6	10·8	27·5
1937	27·9	10·8	10·6	26·9
1938	26·2	9·0	9·5	25·2
1939	28·1	12·9	11·9	28·2
·940	31·0	15·9	15·1	32·2

SOURCE: Department of Commerce, *National Income Supplement to Survey of Current Business, 1951.*

† P is obtained from gross profits by deducting all direct taxes. *Direct* taxes on wages and salaries were very small in the period considered.

modified as compared with its basic concept. In addition to gross investment, export surplus and budget deficit, it here includes brokerage fees. In the United States statistics these are included in consumption. However, as this is a typical capital expenditure which is not closely related to income, it is proper here to consider it on a par with investment. As a deflator for both series the price index implicit in the deflation of gross national product of the private sector is used.†

Before establishing the correlation between P and I' it was necessary to determine the time lag, ω. This was complicated by the fact that some trend also appeared to be involved in the relation between P and I'. In order to circumvent this difficulty, the trend was approximately eliminated by taking into consideration the first differences ΔP and $\Delta I'$. From correlating these differences it appeared that the best fit is obtained for a time lag of about three months.

In view of this, P was correlated with $I'_{t-\frac{1}{4}}$, i.e. with I' shifted three months back by means of interpolation. Thus, $I'_{t-\frac{1}{4}}$ was obtained by taking three-fourths of I' in a given year and one-fourth of I' in the preceding year. To allow for trend a double correlation was established of P with $I'_{t-\frac{1}{4}}$ and the time t (counted in years from the middle of the period 1929–40, i.e. from the beginning of 1935). The regression equation is:

$$P_t = 1\cdot34I'_{t-\frac{1}{4}} + 13\cdot4 - 0\cdot13t$$

The value of profits calculated from this equation are given for comparison with actual profits in Table 7.1. The correlation is very close. The double correlation coefficient is 0·986.

If there were no saving out of wages and salaries the coefficient of $I'_{t-\frac{1}{4}}$ would be equal $1/(1-q)$ in equation (7.4″). In this case we should have for q, which is the coefficient indicating what part of an increment of profits will be directed to consumption:

$$\frac{1}{1-q} = 1\cdot34; \; q = 0\cdot25$$

† For details of the calculation of P and I' see Statistical Appendix, Notes 7 and 8.

This would mean that only 25 per cent of additional profits would be devoted to consumption and 75 per cent to savings. Actually, the coefficient q will be larger, because part of savings comes from labour income. However, q is unlikely to exceed 30 per cent by very much.

The trend coefficient is negative, which is probably mainly accounted for by the fact that, as a result of the Great Depression, profits in the 'thirties were much lower than profits in the preceding decade, and that this long-run fall in profits could have caused a decline in the constant, A, during the period considered. In other words, capitalists' standard of living was declining as a result of the long-run slump in profits.

8. DETERMINATION OF NATIONAL INCOME AND CONSUMPTION

[(1939) 1954]

INTRODUCTION

In Chapter 6 the relative share of wages and salaries in the national income was investigated and in the last chapter the relationship between profits and I', the sum of investment, export surplus and budget deficit was established. The combination of the results of these two inquiries will enable us to establish a relation between the national income and I'. Thus, in the special case where foreign trade and the government budget are balanced, the national income will be related to investment I.

The formula for the relative share of wages and salaries in the gross income of the private sector established in Chapter 6 (p. 76) is as follows:

$$\frac{V}{Y} = \alpha + \frac{B}{Y}$$

where V is the 'real' wage and salary bill, and Y is the 'real' gross income of the private sector. The coefficient α is positive and < 1 and the constant B, which is subject to long-run changes, is also positive. The difference between Y and V is gross profits before taxes π. (In the preceding chapter P represented gross profits *after* taxes.) We thus have:

$$\frac{Y-\pi}{Y} = \alpha + \frac{B}{Y}$$

or

$$Y = \frac{\pi + B}{1 - \alpha} \qquad (8.1)$$

Dynamics of capitalist economy

For an understanding of the subsequent discussion a few words should be added about the difference between the gross *national product* and the gross *income* of the *private sector*, Y. The difference between the gross *national* product and the gross *private* product is accounted for by the government product as measured by payments to government employees. The difference between the value of gross private *product* and the gross *income* of the private sector, Y, is accounted for by indirect taxes which are included in the value of the private product.† Thus, the difference between gross national product and the gross income of the private sector consists of payments to government employees and indirect taxes.

NATIONAL PRODUCT, PROFITS, AND INVESTMENT IN A SIMPLIFIED MODEL

We shall discuss the problem of determination of national product or income first with respect to the simplified model considered at the beginning of Chapter 7. We assumed there a closed system and a negligible government revenue and expenditure. As a result gross national product is equal to the sum of private investment and consumption. We also abstracted from workers' savings. For such a model, as we have seen, formula (7.4′) relating profits after taxes, P, to investment, I (see p. 88), is valid:

$$P_t = \frac{I_{t-\omega} + A}{1 - q} \tag{7.4′}$$

where $1 > q > 0$ and $A > 0$. Since tax revenue is negligible, profits before and after tax may be taken as identical. Gross national product and gross private income of the private sector, Y, may also be taken as identical since both payments to government employees and indirect taxation are negligible. We thus have the following equations for the determination of

† Since the gross income of the private sector, Y, is taken here before direct taxation, Y includes *direct* taxes.

Determination of national income

gross national product:

$$Y_t = \frac{P_t + B}{1 - \alpha} \tag{8.1'}$$

$$P_t = \frac{I_{t-\omega} + A}{1 - q} \tag{7.4'}$$

It is clear that the gross income or product, Y_t, is fully determined by investment, $I_{t-\omega}$.

Since equation (8.1') reflects the factors determining the distribution of national income we can also say: the gross income, Y_t, is pushed up to a point at which profits out of it, as determined by the 'distribution factors', correspond to the level of investment $I_{t-\omega}$. The role of the 'distribution factors' is thus to determine income or product on the basis of profits which are in turn determined by investment. The mechanism of such determination of income has already been described in Chapter 7 (see pp. 80–81).

It follows directly that changes in the distribution of income occur not by way of a change in profits, P, but through a change in gross income or product, Y. Imagine, for instance, that as a result of the increase in the degree of monopoly the relative share of profits in the gross income rises. Profits will remain unchanged because they continue to be determined by investment which depends on past investment decisions, but the real wages and salaries and the gross income or product will fall. The level of income or product will decline to the point at which the higher relative share of profits yields the same absolute level of profits. In our equations it will be reflected as follows: the increase in the degree of monopoly will cause a fall of the coefficient, α.† As a result, a lower level of income or product, Y_t, will correspond to a given level of investment, $I_{t-\omega}$.

† According to equation (6.2), α is that part of the relative share of wages and salaries in income Y which is independent of the level of Y; the other part B/Y stands for the influence of the overhead element in salaries.

CHANGES IN INVESTMENT AND CONSUMPTION
IN A SIMPLIFIED MODEL

Given the relations between profits and investment and gross income and profits, as expressed by equations $(7.4')$ and $(8.1')$, any change in investment causes a definite change in income. A rise in investment by $\Delta I_{t-\omega}$ causes with a time lag a rise in profits by:

$$\Delta P_t = \frac{\Delta I_{t-\omega}}{1-q}$$

Moreover, a rise in profits by ΔP causes a rise in the gross income or product by:

$$\Delta Y_t = \frac{\Delta P_t}{1-\alpha}$$

or

$$\Delta Y_t = \frac{\Delta I_{t-\omega}}{(1-\alpha)(1-q)}$$

It should be remembered that q is the coefficient indicating that part of ΔP, an increment of profits, which will be devoted to consumption; and that α is the coefficient indicating that part of ΔY, an increment in the gross income, which goes to wages and salaries. Both $1-q$ and $1-\alpha$ are < 1, so that $\Delta Y_t > \Delta I_{t-\omega}$. In other words, gross income or product increases more than investment owing to the effect of the rise in investment upon capitalists' consumption {factor $1/(1-q)$} and upon workers' income {factor $1/(1-\alpha)$}. Since workers' consumption is here assumed to be equal to their income, this means that income increases more than investment because of the influence of the increase in investment upon capitalists' and workers' consumption.† During a slump the fall in investment also causes a reduction in consumption so that the fall in employment is larger than that arising directly from the curtailment of investment activity.

† It should be noticed that equation $(8.1')$ which reflects the price–cost relationship, is based on the condition of elastic supply postulated in Part I. If the supply of consumption goods is inelastic an increase in investment will not result in a rise in the volume of consumption but merely in an increase in the prices of consumption goods (cf. footnote to p. 81). In the subsequent argument we continue to assume, in line with Part I, the condition of elastic supply.

In order to bring into focus the nature of this process in the capitalist economy it is useful to consider what the effect of a reduction in investment in a socialist system would be. The workers released from the production of investment goods would be employed in consumption goods industries. The increased supply of these goods would be absorbed by means of a reduction in their prices. Since profits of the socialist industries would be equal to investment, prices would have to be reduced to the point where the decline in profits would be equal to the fall in the value of investment. In other words, full employment would be maintained through the reduction of prices in relation to costs. In the capitalist system, however, the price–cost relationship, as reflected in equation (8.1'), is maintained and profits fall by the same amount as investment plus capitalists' consumption through the reduction in output and employment. It is indeed paradoxical that, while the apologists of capitalism usually consider the 'price mechanism' to be the great advantage of the capitalist system, price flexibility proves to be a characteristic feature of the socialist economy.†

Up to this point we have been considering the relation between the *absolute* changes of investment, I, profits, P, and gross income or product, Y. It is of interest also to compare their *proportionate* changes. Let us go back for this purpose to equations (7.4') and (8.1'). It should be remembered that the constant A, the stable part of capitalists' consumption, and the constant B, the stable part of salaries, are positive. It follows that profits, P, change proportionately less in the course of the business cycle than investment, I, and that the same is true of gross income, Y, in relation to profits, P. Consequently, the relative changes of gross income, Y, are smaller than those of investment, I.

Since in our model gross income or product, Y, is equal to the sum of investment and consumption, the relative changes of

---

† It should be noticed that in an expanding socialist economy a reduction in the price–cost ratio will reflect a relative rather than an absolute shift from investment to consumption.

consumption are smaller than those of gross income. For, if one component (investment) varies proportionately more than the sum (gross income or product) the other component (consumption) must vary proportionately less than the sum. It follows directly that investment varies proportionately more than consumption, or in other words, that it falls in relation to consumption during the slump and rises during the boom.

THE GENERAL CASE

Let us now drop the assumption that government expenditure and revenue are negligible. For the time being we may continue to assume that foreign trade and the government budget are balanced and that workers do not save. Thus, equation (7.4′):

$$P_t = \frac{I_{t-\omega} + A}{1 - q} \qquad (7.4')$$

still holds good but profits before taxes, π, are no longer identical with profits after taxes, P. We shall assume that the tax system is given and that the relation between 'real' profits before taxes, π, and 'real' profits after taxes, P, can be expressed approximately by a linear function. We are then able to substitute for formula (8.1′) the equation:

$$Y_t = \frac{P_t + B'}{1 - \alpha} \qquad (8.1'')$$

where the constant α' and B' do not depend merely on the factors underlying the distribution of national income, but are influenced also by the effect of the tax system on profits. From these two equations it is apparent that gross income of the private sector Y is again determined—with a time lag—by investment I. To an increment in investment $\Delta I_{t-\omega}$ there corresponds an increment in gross income:

$$\Delta Y_t = \frac{\Delta I_{t-\omega}}{(1 - \alpha')(1 - q)}$$

ΔY is here again larger than ΔI. This, however, is accounted for not only by the increase in capitalists' and workers' consumption following the rise in investment, but also by the larger volume of direct taxes which they pay out of increased income.

Passing now to the general case where foreign trade and the government budget are not necessarily balanced and workers' savings are not necessarily zero, we have (see p. 89):

$$P_t = \frac{I'_{t-\omega} + A'}{1 - q} \qquad (7.4''')$$

where I' is the sum of investment, export surplus and budget deficit, and where q' and A' differ from q and A in equation $(7.4')$ in that they reflect workers' savings. The shape of equation $(8.1'')$ is unchanged:

$$Y_t = \frac{P_t + B'}{1 - \alpha'} \qquad (8.1'')$$

These two equations determine Y_t in terms of $I'_{t-\omega}$. The increment in Y_t corresponding to the increment of $I'_{t-\omega}$ is:

$$\Delta Y_t = \frac{\Delta I'_{t-\omega}}{(1 - \alpha')(1 - q')}$$

The determination of consumption is much more complicated than in our simplified model where consumption was the difference between Y and I. In the general case consumption is the difference between aggregate income after tax and savings. Now savings are equal to I', the sum of investment, export surplus and budget deficit. Aggregate income after tax is not equal here to Y. Indeed, the latter is the gross income of the private sector which does not include the income of government employees or government transfer payments and is *before* direct taxes. Aggregate income after tax is equal to Y, plus the income of government employees and government transfer payments and minus all direct taxes. It follows that consumption is equal to $Y - I'$ minus direct taxes, plus income of government employees plus transfers. It is obvious that consumption cannot be fully determined in terms of I' by the above equations which permit the determination of $Y - I'$ only.

We shall now estimate the coefficients of the relation between Y and I' for the United States in the period 1929–41. On p. 76 we established for that period the following equation for the relative share of the wage and salary bill, V, in the gross income of the private sector, Y:

$$\frac{V}{Y}\,100 = 42\cdot5 + \frac{707}{Y} + 0\cdot11t$$

where the time, t, is counted from 1935.

Taking into consideration that profits before tax $\pi = Y - V$ we obtain

$$\frac{Y - \pi}{Y} = 0\cdot425 + \frac{7\cdot07}{Y} + 0\cdot0011t$$

From this equation Y can be calculated on the basis of π. In Table 8·1 are given the actual 'real' values of Y and π† and the

TABLE 8.1 *Gross income of the private sector and profits in the United States, 1929–41*

Year	Gross income of the private sector Y	Profits before taxes π	Calculated gross income of the private sector
	(Billions of dollars at 1939 prices)		
1929	74·1	37·0	75·5
1930	65·9	31·4	66·2
1931	59·3	26·7	58·2
1932	48·0	20·2	47·0
1933	46·9	19·8	46·2
1934	51·9	22·8	51·6
1935	57·7	27·3	60·0
1936	65·5	30·5	65·2
1937	69·0	32·2	67·9
1938	64·3	30·1	65·7
1939	68·8	32·0	69·0
1940	75·9	36·3	76·1
1941	89·6	43·6	89·0

SOURCE: Department of Commerce, *National Income Supplement to Survey of Current Business, 1951*. For details see *Statistical Appendix*, Notes 6 and 7.

† As deflator, the index implicit in the deflation of the gross product of the private sector by the U.S. Department of Commerce was used again.

calculated value of Y. The correlation between the actual and calculated Y is extremely close. The coefficient of correlation is 0·995.

If we drop the trend component in the above equation we obtain:

$$Y = 1·74\pi + 12·2$$

which is the counterpart of equation (8.1). We still have to take taxation of profits into consideration if we are to obtain the relation of Y to profits after tax, P. For this purpose we correlate 'real' profits before and after taxes (P was given above in Table 8.1) and obtain a regression equation which, we may assume, characterizes the tax system prevailing in that period.† This relationship between π and P permits us to express Y in terms of profits after tax, P. We thus have as a counterpart of equation (9″):

$$Y_t = 2·03P_t + 10·4$$

The relation between P and I' for the same period was established above (p. 91). Disregarding the trend component we have as a counterpart of equation (8‴):

$$P_t = 1·34I'_{t-\frac{1}{4}} + 13·4$$

From these two equations we obtain:

$$Y_t = 2·72I'_{t-\frac{1}{4}} + 37·7$$

The increment of Y_t, which corresponds, with a time lag, to an increment of $I'_{t-\frac{1}{4}}$ is:

$$\Delta Y_t = 2·72\,\Delta I'_{t-\frac{1}{4}}$$

Thus, *absolute* changes in Y are considerably larger than those in I'. At the same time, according to the preceding equation, *proportionate* changes in Y are smaller than those in I'.

† We take into consideration here the period 1929–40 rather than 1929–41. The regression equation is: $P = 0·86\pi + 0·9$. The correlation is quite close which results from the fact that the system of direct taxes was fairly stable over the period considered. Taxes were increased considerably, however, in 1941. (For details see Statistical Appendix, Note 9.)

Dynamics of capitalist economy

As stated above (p. 94) the gross income of the private sector, Y, is not equal to the gross product of that sector. In order to pass from the former to the latter it is necessary to add indirect taxes of all kinds, such as excise and custom duties or employers' contributions to social insurance. If we denote the 'real' gross product or output of the private sector by O and the 'real' value of the aggregate indirect taxes by E we have:†

$$O = Y + E$$

As was shown above, Y is determined—with a time lag—by the sum of investment, export surplus and budget deficit I' or by investment I if foreign trade and the budget are balanced. In order to determine the gross product of the private sector it is necessary to make some assumptions about E. The relative fluctuations of E in the course of the business cycle are usually much smaller than those of gross income, Y, for the following reasons: (*a*) indirect taxes are frequently levied on necessities or semi-necessities, the consumption of which fluctuates much less than Y; (*b*) the rates are frequently fixed in money and not *ad valorem* so that the real value of such rates increases when prices fall. For the sake of simplicity we shall assume in the theory of business cycle developed below that E is a constant.

For the determination of the output of the private sector, O, in terms of the sum of investment, export surplus and budget deficit, I', we now have:

$$O_t = Y_t + E \tag{8.2}$$

$$Y_t = \frac{P_t + B'}{1 - \alpha'} \tag{8.1''}$$

$$P_t = \frac{I'_{t-\omega} + A'}{1 - q'} \tag{7.4'''}$$

† We imagine Y and E to be deflated by the same price index as O, i.e. by the index of *market* prices.

It follows directly that an increment of $I'_{t-\omega}$ determines an increment of O_t:

$$\Delta O_t = \frac{\Delta I'_{t-\omega}}{(1 - \alpha')(1 - q')}$$

On the assumption that E is a constant, O will show smaller proportionate changes than Y. As the relative changes of Y in the course of the cycle are smaller than those of I' it follows that this is even more true of O. Thus, if foreign trade and the budget are balanced so that $I' = I$, it can be said that the gross product of the private sector O fluctuates less than investment I.

LONG-RUN CHANGES IN INVESTMENT AND INCOME

It has been shown above that the relative changes of investment, I (or rather of the sum of investment, export surplus and budget deficit, I', which is equal to savings) in the course of the business cycle are greater than those of gross income or output of the private sector. However, this is not necessarily the case in the long run.

The discrepancy in fluctuations of I' and Y or O in the course of the business cycle depends mainly on two factors: (*a*) that capitalists' consumption fluctuates less than profits; and (*b*) that wages plus salaries fluctuate less than gross income, Y. However, capitalists' consumption need not increase more slowly than profits in the course of the long-run growth of an economy. Indeed, the stable part of capitalists' consumption, A (see p. 86), may rise in the long run proportionately with profits, P. In the same way the stable part of wages and salaries, B, which reflects the overhead element in salaries (see p. 76) may also rise in the long run proportionately with income, Y. Thus, in the long run, investment and income may not show disproportionate changes as they do in the course of the business cycle.

It appears that in the United States, in the period 1870–1914, the long-run changes in investment and income were in fact roughly proportional. In Table 8.2 is given the ratio of 'gross capital formation' to 'gross national income' for that period by decades according to Kuznets. This ratio remained fairly stable.

TABLE 8.2 *Ratio of 'gross capital formation' to 'gross national income' in the United States, 1869–1913*

Years	(%)
1869–1878	18·9
1874–1883	19·0
1879–1888	19·2
1884–1893	20·8
1889–1898	16·3
1894–1903	21·1
1899–1908	20·1
1904–1913	19·8

SOURCE: S. Kuznets, *National Product since 1869*, New York, 1946.

Although both the numerator and denominator differ in concept from I' and Y,† it is virtually certain that in the period considered I' and Y moved roughly proportionately to the 'gross capital formation' and to the 'gross national income' respectively. The stability of the ratio of I' to Y does not necessarily mean that both the distribution of income and the proportion of consumption out of profits remained constant because there might have been compensating changes in these factors. In any case the above is not meant to suggest that the long-run stability of the ratio of savings to income is an economic law, but merely to show that there is a possibility of such a relationship.

† I' = 'gross capital formation' minus public investment plus budget deficit.
  Y = 'gross national income' minus public investment plus budget deficit minus income of government employees.
  The differences in question are small in the period considered and therefore proportionality in the change between I' and 'gross capital formation' and between Y and 'gross national income' may be assumed.

9. ENTREPRENEURIAL CAPITAL AND INVESTMENT

[(1937) 1954]

THE SIZE OF THE FIRM AND ENTREPRENEURIAL CAPITAL

Two factors are usually mentioned as limiting the size of a firm: (1) dis-economies of a large scale; and (2) limitations of market, the expansion of which would require unprofitable price reductions or increases in selling costs. The first of these factors seems to be rather unrealistic. It has no technological basis because, although every plant has an optimum size, it is still possible to have two, three, or more plants. The argument with respect to difficulties of management arising out of large-scale enterprise also seems doubtful since adequate measures of decentralization can always be introduced to meet this problem. The limitation of the size of the firm by the market for its products is real enough but it leaves unexplained the existence of large and small firms in the same industry.

There is, however, another factor which is of decisive importance in limiting the size of a firm: the amount of the entrepreneurial capital, i.e. the amount of capital owned by the firm. The access of a firm to the capital market, or in other words the amount of rentier capital it may hope to obtain, is determined to a large extent by the amount of its entrepreneurial capital. It would be impossible for a firm to borrow capital above a certain level determined by the amount of its entrepreneurial capital. If, for instance, a firm should attempt to float a bond issue which was too large in terms of its entrepreneurial capital, this issue would not be subscribed in full. Even if the firm should undertake to issue the bonds at a higher rate of interest than that prevailing, the sale of bonds might not be improved since the higher rate in itself might raise misgivings with regard to the future solvency of the firm.

In addition, many firms will not use to the full the potentialities of the capital market because of the 'increasing risk' involved in expansion. Indeed, some firms may even keep their investment at a level below that of the entrepreneurial capital, a part of which may be held in securities. A firm considering expansion must face the fact that, given the amount of the entrepreneurial capital, the risk increases with the amount invested. The greater the investment in relation to the entrepreneurial capital, the greater is the reduction of the entrepreneur's income in the event of an unsuccessful business venture. Suppose, for instance, that an entrepreneur fails to make any return on his business. Now, if only a part of his capital is invested in business and a part is held in first-rate bonds, he will still derive some net income from his capital. If all of his capital is invested his income will be zero, while, if he has borrowed, he will suffer a net loss which, if it continues long enough, must drive his business out of existence. It is clear that the heavier the borrowing the greater will be the danger of such a contingency.

The size of a firm thus appears to be circumscribed by the amount of its entrepreneurial capital both through its influence on the capacity to borrow capital and through its effect on the degree of risk. The variety in the size of enterprises in the same industry at a given time can be easily explained in terms of differences in entrepreneurial capital. A firm with a large entrepreneurial capital could obtain funds for a large investment whereas a firm with a small entrepreneurial capital could not. Differences in the position of firms arising out of differences in their entrepreneurial capital are further enhanced by the fact that firms below a certain size have no access whatever to the capital market.

It follows from the above that the expansion of the firm depends on its accumulation of capital out of current profits.

Entrepreneurial capital

This will enable the firm to undertake new investment without encountering the obstacles of the limited capital market or 'increasing risk'. Not only can savings out of current profits be directly invested in the business, but this increase in the firm's capital will make it possible to contract new loans.

THE PROBLEM OF JOINT-STOCK COMPANIES

Legitimate doubt may arise as to whether the above limitations to investment are applicable in the case of joint-stock companies. If a company issues bonds or debentures the situation is not materially altered. The greater the issue the more are dividends impaired in the event of an unsuccessful business venture. The position is similar in the case of an issue of preference shares (the fixed return on which is paid from profit before any return accrues to ordinary shares). But what about an issue of ordinary shares? Prima facie it would seem that no limits are set to such an issue, but in fact there are quite a few restraining factors.

(*a*) It should first be stated that a joint-stock company is not a 'brotherhood of shareholders' but is managed by a controlling group of big shareholders while the rest of the shareholders do not differ from holders of bonds with a flexible rate of interest. Now, this group, if it is to continue to exercise control, cannot sell an unlimited number of shares to the 'public'. It is true that this 'difficulty' may be partly overcome, for instance, by building up holding companies.† Nevertheless, the problem of the maintenance of control by top shareholders exerts *some* restraining influence upon issues to the 'public'.

(*b*) There is a risk that the investment financed by an issue of shares may not increase company profits proportionately as

---

† A group possessing 51 per cent of shares of a company starts a new company to hold their shares. The group retains 51 per cent of the shares of the new company and sells 49 per cent to the public. It now controls the holding company and through it the old company with only about 26 per cent of the capital of the latter, while it has about 25 per cent of this capital in cash which it is free to invest in a new share issue of the old company.

much as the issue increased the share and reserve capital. If the rate of return on the new investment does not at least equal the old rate of profits, then the dividends of the old shareholders in general and of the controlling group in particular will be 'squeezed'. Risk of this type is, of course, the greater the larger the new issue. This is, therefore, another case of 'increasing risk'.

(c) Share issues are restrained by the limited market for shares of a given company. The 'public' tend to distribute their risks by holding a variety of shares. It will be impossible, therefore, to place more than a limited amount of new shares at a price which would be reasonable from the point of view of the old shareholders. For the latter the price at which new shares are sold is of crucial importance. Indeed, if this price is 'too low' in relation to expected profits, a situation similar to that considered under (b) will arise. The new issue will not increase the earning capacity of the company proportionately as much as its share and reserve capital and this will result in a 'squeezing' of the dividends of the old shareholders.

All this points to the fact that a joint-stock company also has definite limitations to its expansion. This expansion depends, as in the case of a family concern, on the accumulation of capital out of current profits. This increase in the entrepreneurial capital, however, is not confined to the undistributed profits of the company. Subscriptions of share issues by the controlling group which are closely connected with the group's 'personal' savings should be considered as another form of accumulation of entrepreneurial capital.

The 'internal' accumulation of capital provides resources which can be 'ploughed back' into the business. Moreover, such an accumulation facilitates new issues of shares to the 'public' because it helps to overcome the obstacles enumerated above. (a) When the accumulation takes the form of subscriptions to share issues by the controlling group, it permits the issue of a certain amount of shares to the 'public' without infringing upon the command of the group over the majority of shares. (b) A growth in the size of the firm through 'internal accumulation of capital decreases the risk involved in issuing a given amount of shares to the 'public' to finance new investment. (*c*) An increase in the capital of the company without recourse to the 'public' will tend to widen the capital market for the shares of that company since, in general, the larger a company is the more important will its role in the share market be.

CONCLUDING REMARKS

The limitation of the size of the firm by the availability of entrepreneurial capital goes to the very heart of the capitalist system. Many economists assume, at least in their abstract theories, a state of business democracy where anybody endowed with entrepreneurial ability can obtain capital for starting a business venture. This picture of the activities of the 'pure' entrepreneur is, to put it mildly, unrealistic. The most important prerequisite for becoming an entrepreneur is the *ownership* of capital.

The above considerations are of great importance for the theory of determination of investment. One of the important factors of investment decisions is the accumulation of firms' capital out of current profits. We shall deal with this subject in detail in the next chapter.†

† The problems discussed here are also of considerable importance for the theory of concentration of capital: cf. J. Steindl, 'Capitalist Enterprise and Risk', *Oxford Economic Papers*, March 1945.

10. DETERMINANTS OF INVESTMENT

[(1943) 1954]

DETERMINANTS OF FIXED CAPITAL INVESTMENT DECISIONS

Our problem here is to find the determinants of the *rate* of investment decisions, i.e. the amount of investment decisions *per unit of time*. Investment decisions in a given period, determined by certain factors operating in that period, are followed by actual investment with a time lag. The time lag is largely due to the period of construction, but also reflects such factors as delayed entrepreneurial reactions. If the amount of fixed capital investment decisions per unit of time is denoted by D, and investment in fixed capital by F, we shall have the relation:

$$F_{t+\tau} = D_t \qquad (10.1)$$

where the lag, τ, is the horizontal distance between the time curve of investment decisions per unit of time, D, and the time curve of investment in fixed capital, F.†

We shall approach the problem of the determinants of fixed capital investment decisions as follows. If we consider the rate of investment decisions in a short period we can assume that at the beginning of this period the firms have pushed their investment plans up to a point where they cease to be profitable either because of the limited market for the firm's products or because of 'increasing risk' and limitation of the capital market. New investment decisions will thus be made only if in the

---

† It should be noticed that investment decisions are not strictly irrevocable. The cancellation of investment orders, although involving considerable loss, can and does take place. This is a factor, therefore, which disturbs the relationship between investment decisions and investment as described by equation (10.1).

period considered, changes in the economic situation take place which extend the boundaries set to investment plans by those factors. We shall take into consideration three broad categories of such changes in the given period: (*a*) gross accumulation of capital by firms out of current profits, i.e. their current gross savings; and (*b*) changes in profits and changes in the stock of fixed capital. Let us examine these factors in more detail.

The first factor has been dealt with in a general way in the preceding chapter. Investment decisions are closely related to 'internal' accumulation of capital, i.e. to the gross savings of firms. There will be a tendency to use these savings for investment, and, in addition, investment may be financed by new outside funds on the strength of the accumulation of entrepreneurial capital. The gross savings of firms thus extend the boundaries set to investment plans by the limited capital market and the factor of 'increasing risk'.

The gross savings of firms consist, strictly speaking, of depreciation and undistributed profits. We shall include with these, however, the 'personal savings' of the controlling groups invested in their own companies through subscriptions to new share issues. This concept of gross savings of firms is thus somewhat vague. We shall get around this difficulty by assuming that the gross savings of firms as conceived above are related to total gross private savings (*inter alia* as a result of the correlation between profits and national income, see p. 93 above). On this assumption the rate of capital investment decisions, D, is an increasing function of total gross savings, S. (We imagine that investment decisions and investment are in real terms— i.e. their values are deflated by the index of prices of investment goods. Thus, it follows directly that gross savings also have to be deflated by the index of prices of investment goods.)

Another factor which influences the rate of investment decisions is the increase in profits per unit of time. A rise in profits from the beginning to the end of the period considered renders attractive certain projects which were previously considered unprofitable and thus permits an extension of the boundaries of investment plans in the course of the period. The value of the resulting new investment decisions divided by the length of the period gives us the contribution of the change of profits per unit of time to the rate of investment decisions in the period considered.

When the profitability of new investment projects is being weighed, expected profits are considered in relation to the value of the new capital equipment. Thus, profits are taken in relation to the current prices of investment goods. We can allow for this factor by deflating profits by the price index of investment goods. In other words, if we denote aggregate gross profits after taxes deflated by the price of investment goods by P,† we can say that *ceteris paribus* the rate of investment decisions, D, is an increasing function of $\Delta P/\Delta t$.

Finally, the net increment of capital equipment per unit of time affects adversely the rate of investment decisions, i.e. without this effect the rate of investment decisions would be higher. Indeed, an increase in the volume of capital equipment if profits, P, are constant means a reduction in the rate of profit. Just as an increase in profits within the period considered renders additional investment projects attractive, so an accumulation of capital equipment tends to restrict the boundaries of investment plans. This effect is most easily seen in the case where new enterprises enter the field and thereby render investment plans of the established firms less attractive. If we denote the value of the stock of capital equipment deflated by appropriate prices by K we can say that the rate of investment decisions, D, is *ceteris paribus* a decreasing function of $\Delta K/\Delta t$.

To sum up: the rate of investment decisions, D, is, as a first approximation, an increasing function of gross savings, S, and of the rate of change in aggregate profits, $\Delta P/\Delta t$, and a decreasing function of the rate of change in the stock of capital

† The concept of 'real' gross profits, P, in Chapters 3, 4 and 5 differs from the present one in that there the price index implicit in the deflation of the gross product of the private sector was used as deflator.

equipment, $\Delta K/\Delta t$. Assuming, moreover, a linear relation we have:

$$D = aS + b\frac{\Delta P}{\Delta t} - c\frac{\Delta K}{\Delta t} + d \qquad (10.2)$$

where d is a constant subject to long-run changes, in particular technical progress. As according to equation (15):

$$F_{t+\tau} = D_t$$

we also have for investment in fixed capital at time $t+\tau$:

$$F_{t+\tau} = aS_t + b\frac{\Delta P_t}{\Delta t} - c\frac{\Delta K_t}{\Delta t} + d \qquad (10.2')$$

FACTORS NOT TAKEN INTO CONSIDERATION

It may be questioned why changes in the rate of interest, which have an opposite effect to changes in profits, were not considered as a co-determinant of investment decisions. This simplification is based on the fact that the long-term rate of interest does not show marked cyclical fluctuations.[†]

It is true that the yields of business debentures sometimes increase appreciably during depressions because of crises of confidence. The omission of this factor does not invalidate the above theory since the rise in the yields of the securities in question works in the same direction as the fall in profits (although it is of much less significance). Thus, this effect may be roughly accounted for in the discussion of the business cycle by a somewhat higher coefficient b in equation (10.2).

It is still necessary, however, to consider the problem raised by the fluctuations of share yields, that is, of the ratios of current dividends to share prices. The movement of yields of preference shares shows very much the same pattern as that of the yields of debentures and may be taken into consideration in the same way. This is not, however, at least not fully, the case for ordinary shares. Although this factor seems to be in

[†] See for instance M. Kalecki, *The Theory of Economic Dynamics* (London 1954), p. 88.

general of limited importance this is not to deny that it may vitiate to some extent the application of the above theory.

We shall now consider briefly an entirely different factor which was not taken into account in building up equation (10.2), namely, innovations. We assume that innovations, in the sense of gradual adjustments of the equipment of a firm to the current state of technology, are part and parcel of 'ordinary' investment as determined by this formula. The immediate effect of a new invention is discussed in Chapter 15 of my *Theory of Economic Dynamics* in connection with the theory of economic development. It will be seen that there these effects are reflected in the level of d. The same is true of the long-run changes in the rate of interest or in the share yields.

TWO SPECIAL CASES OF THE THEORY

It can be shown that equation (10.2) covers, as special cases, some of the existing theories of investment decisions.

Let us first assume that the coefficients a and c are equal to zero so that the equation is reduced to

$$D = b \frac{\Delta P}{\Delta t} + D$$

Let us assume in addition that d is equal to depreciation. It follows that net investment is determined by the rate of change in 'real' profits. This case corresponds roughly to the so-called acceleration principle. It is true that this principle establishes a relationship between net investment and the rate of change in output rather than in profits and that the theoretical foundations are different from those given above, but the final results are much the same because of the inter-relationship between 'real' profits and aggregate output (see Chapter 8).

With respect to the theoretical problem, it would appear to be more realistic to base the 'acceleration principle' on the grounds suggested above (see p. 111) than to deduce it from the necessity of expanding capacity in order to increase output.

It is well known that large reserve capacities exist, at least throughout a considerable part of the cycle, and that output, therefore, may increase without an actual increase in existing capacities. But, whatever the basis of the 'acceleration principle' may be, it is inadequate not only because it does not take into consideration the other determinants of investment decisions examined above, but also because it does not agree with the facts. In the course of the business cycle the highest rate of increase in output will be somewhere close to the medium position (see Fig. 10.1). It would follow from the 'acceleration

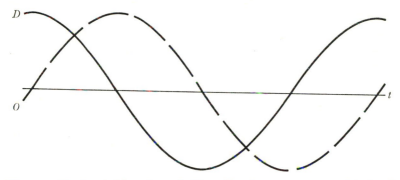

FIG. 10.1. Fixed capital investment decisions, *D*, and aggregate output, *O* (reduced to the same amplitude), according to the 'acceleration principle'.

principle' that the highest level of investment decisions would come into existence at that time. This, however, is unrealistic. Indeed, it would mean that the time lag between investment decisions and aggregate output would be about one-fourth of the business cycle or 1·5 to 2·5 years. As it is difficult to assume that the time lag between investment decisions and actual investment would be more than one year,† it would mean that the actual investment in fixed capital would 'lead' output by 0·5 to 1·5 years. The available data do not substantiate such a lag. This will be seen, for instance, from Fig. 10.2 where the time curves of investment in fixed capital and output (gross

† Cf. M. Kalecki, *The Theory of Economic Dynamics* (London 1954), p. 109.

product of the private sector) are given for the United States for the period 1929–40. It appears that no appreciable time lag is discernible. The regression equation, patterned on our equation (10.2′), which can be obtained for United States investment in fixed capital for this period,† also does not conform at all to the 'acceleration principle'.

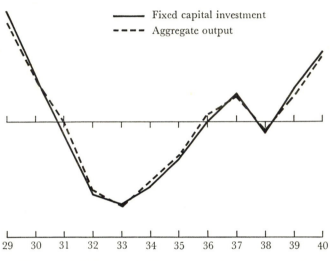

FIG. 10.2. Fluctuations in fixed capital investment and gross product of the private sector, United States, 1929–40. The time curves are reduced to the same amplitude and the intervening trend is eliminated. (For details see Statistical Appendix, Note 10, below.)

We obtain the second special case of our theory by assuming that a given amount of new savings affects investment decisions to an equal extent, that is, by assuming that a is equal to 1. We also assume that the constant d is equal to 0. Thus, we have:

$$D = S + b\frac{\Delta P}{\Delta t} - c\frac{\Delta K}{\Delta t}$$

If in addition the assumption is made that inventories are stable throughout the cycle and that the export surplus and the

† See M. Kalecki, *The Theory of Economic Dynamics* (London 1954), p. 112.

budget deficit are both equal to zero, it follows that savings, S, are equal to actual investment in fixed capital, F (because savings are equal to investment in fixed capital and inventories plus export surplus plus budget deficit). We thus obtain:

$$D = F + b \frac{\Delta P}{\Delta t} - c \frac{\Delta K}{\Delta t}$$

and taking into consideration that $F_t = D_{t-\tau}$

$$D_t = D_{t-\tau} + b \frac{\Delta P_t}{\Delta_t} - c \frac{\Delta K_t}{\Delta_t}$$

or

$$D_t - D_{t-\tau} = b \frac{\Delta P_t}{\Delta t} - c \frac{\Delta K_t}{\Delta t}$$

Now it is clear from the last equation that if profits, P, and the stock of capital equipment, K, are constant, so is the rate of investment decisions, D (because $D_t = D_{t-\tau}$). When profits increase to a new level, so does D (because during the period when P is increasing $D_t > D_{t-\tau}$). When the stock of capital equipment, K, rises to a new level, D declines (because during the period when K is increasing $D_t < D_{t-\tau}$). If follows that the rate of investment decisions is an increasing function of the level of profits and a decreasing function of the stock of capital equipment. This is the relationship which was the basis of the theory of the business cycle given in my *Essays on the Theory of Economic Fluctuations*. Thus this theory also appears to be a special case of the present one.

It is sometimes assumed that the relationship obtained here as a special case is operative under all conditions, on the following grounds. The expected rate of profit may be assumed to be an increasing function of 'real' current profits and a decreasing function of the stock of capital equipment. It is further considered obvious that the higher the expected rate of profits the higher the level of investment in fixed capital will be.† The latter, however, is plausible only at first glance. The relation ceases to be obvious when it is remembered that we

† Such was also my conception in my early papers (see Chapters 1 and 3).

consider here the amount of investment decisions *per unit of time*. If a certain level of the rate of profits is maintained for some time, then the firm would make all the investment decisions which correspond to that rate of profits so that after that, unless some new facts came into the picture, no decisions would be forthcoming. It is the full reinvestment of savings coupled with the equality of savings and investment in fixed capital that assures, in the special case considered, the maintenance of the level of investment decisions per unit of time when the rate of profits is constant. But once these fairly rigid assumptions are dropped the theorem ceases to be true and a more general approach based on the equation

$$D = aS + b\frac{\Delta P}{\Delta t} - c\frac{\Delta K}{\Delta t} + d$$

is necessary.

EXAMINATION OF THE FUNDAMENTAL EQUATION

Before proceeding with an examination of the coefficients of equation (10.2′) it will be useful to alter it somewhat. Let us first take into consideration the fact that the rate of change in fixed capital equipment is equal to investment in fixed capital net of depreciation in the same period:

$$\frac{\Delta K}{\Delta t} = F - \delta$$

where δ is depreciation of equipment due to wear and tear and obsolescence. Thus, equation (10.2′) can be written as follows:

$$F_{t+\tau} = aS_t + b\frac{\Delta P_t}{\Delta t} - c(F_t - \delta) + d$$

Let us now transfer $-cF_t$ from the right-hand to the left-hand side of the equation and divide both sides of the equation by $1 + c$:

$$\frac{F_{t+\tau} + cF_t}{1+c} = \frac{a}{1+c}S_t + \frac{b}{1+c}\frac{\Delta P_t}{\Delta t} + \frac{c\delta + d}{1+c}$$

The left-hand side of the equation is then a weighted average of $F_{t+\tau}$ and F_c. We can assume as a good approximation that it is equal to an intermediate value $F_{t+\theta}$ where θ is a time lag less then τ. As c is likely to be a rather small fraction,† θ is of the same order as τ. We can now write:

$$F_{t+\theta} = \frac{a}{1+c} S_t + \frac{b}{1+c} \frac{\Delta P_t}{\Delta t} + \frac{c\delta + d}{1+c}$$

The determinants of investment in fixed capital are thus reduced to past savings and to the past rate of change in profits. The negative effect of an increase in the stock of capital equipment is reflected in the denominator $1+c$. To simplify the form of the equation we shall denote

$$\frac{b}{1+c} = b' \quad \text{and} \quad \frac{c\delta + d}{1+c} = d'$$

No such abbreviation will, however, be introduced for $a/(1+c)$ because its dependence on a and c (the coefficients of savings, S, and of the rate of change in the stock of capital equipment, $\Delta K/\Delta t$, respectively, in the initial equation) is of significance for the subsequent discussion. We thus can write our equation finally in the form

$$F_{t+\theta} = \frac{a}{1+c} S_t + b' \frac{\Delta P_t}{\Delta t} + d' \tag{10.3}$$

We shall now examine the coefficients of this equation. The constant d' is subject to long-run changes.‡ An analysis of the

† Cyclical fluctuations in the stock of capital, K, in percentage terms are rather small. Thus, changes in the rate of profit resulting from this factor are small at well. Consequently, fluctuations in investment in fixed capital are accounted for to a much greater extent by changes in S and $\Delta P/\Delta t$ than by those in $\Delta K/\Delta t$ (although the latter may be of considerable significance in certain phases of the cycle, as will be seen in Chapter 11). In other words, the amplitude of fluctuations in $c(\Delta K/\Delta t)$ is much smaller than that in F. But as $\Delta K/\Delta t$ is the net investment in fixed capital (and the depreciation δ undergoes only slight cyclical fluctuations) this means that c is small as compared with 1.

‡ d' denotes $(c\delta + d)/(1+c)$. On p. 113 d was assumed to be a constant subject to long-run changes. Depreciation, δ, fluctuates only very little in the course of the business cycle, but in the long run it varies in line with the volume of capital equipment.

factors on which these changes depend is given in Chapter 15 of my *Theory of Economic Dynamics*. However, as will be seen below its value is not relevant in a discussion of the business cycle. Nothing can be said on *a priori* basis about the coefficient b', although, as will be seen, its value is of decisive importance in determining the character of cyclical fluctuations. It will thus be necessary to consider a few alternative cases with different values of this coefficient. The only coefficient about which we shall make definite assumptions at this stage is $a/(1+c)$.

The coefficient a, which indicates by how much investment decisions, D, increase as a result of increments in total current savings, S, will be influenced by various factors. First, the increment in the 'internal' savings of the firms which is relevant for investment decisions is smaller than the increment in total saving. This factor in itself would tend to make a less than 1. Another factor works in the same direction. The reinvestment of savings on a *ceteris paribus* basis, that is with constant aggregate profits, may encounter difficulties because the market for the firm's products is limited, and expansion into new spheres of activity involves considerable risk. On the other hand, an increment in 'internal' savings enables the firm to absorb outside funds at a higher rate if investment *is* considered desirable. This factor tends to increase investment decisions by more than the increment in 'internal' savings. These conflicting factors leave us still uncertain about whether a will be greater or less than 1.

The coefficient $a/(1+c)$ is smaller than a because c is positive. According to the above, this reflects the negative influence upon investment decisions of an increasing stock of capital equipment. We shall assume that this coefficient is less than 1 for the following reasons. It will be seen below that with $a/(1+c) > 1$ there would be in fact no business cycle at all (see Chapter 11), and the long-run development of the capitalist economy also would be different from the process we know.† Moreover, the analysis of the United States data for the period 1929–40 yields

† See M. Kalecki, *The Theory of Economic Dynamics* (London 1954), ch. 14.

for $a/(1+c)$ a value significantly less than 1. Since the coefficient c is a rather small fraction (see p. 119 above) $a/(1+c) < 1$ means that a cannot be much higher than 1 (and, of course, it can be $\leqslant 1$).

INVESTMENT IN INVENTORIES

In our analysis of investment in fixed capital we arrived at equation (10.3) which indicates that fixed capital investment decisions are a function both of the level of economic activity and of the rate of change in this level. Indeed, the amount of savings, S, in the equation is associated with the *level* of economic activity, while the rate of increase in profits, $\Delta P/\Delta t$, is related to the *rate of change* in this level. It is for this reason that the 'acceleration principle' which bases itself on the rate of change only is inadequate for the explanation of investment in fixed capital. However, for investment in inventories, the 'acceleration principle' seems to be a reasonable assumption.

It is indeed plausible to assume that the rate of change in the volume of inventories is roughly proportionate to the rate of change in output or the volume of sales. However, empirical investigations of changes in inventories show that here also a significant time lag between cause and effect is clearly discernible. This is accounted for by the fact that a rise in output and sales does not create any immediate need for an increase in inventories, because a part of inventories serves as a reserve and, therefore, it is temporarily possible to increase the velocity of turnover of total inventories. It is only after some time that inventories are adjusted to the new higher level of output. Similarly, when output falls the volume of inventories is accordingly curtailed, but only after a certain delay and in the meantime there is a decline in their velocity of turnover.

There arises the question whether the availability of capital does not play a significant role in investment in inventories as it does in investment in fixed capital. In other words, whether we should not assume that investment in inventories depends not only on the rate of change in output, but on the influx of new savings as well. This, however, does not seem in general to be the case since inventories are semi-liquid assets and short-term credit can be depended upon to finance any expansion in step with output and sales.

In the light of the above we can relate investment in inventories, J, to the rate of change in output of the private sector, $\Delta O/\Delta t$, with a certain time lag. According to the information available this time lag seems to be of a similar order to that involved in fixed capital investment, τ. For the sake of simplicity we shall assume that the inventory time lag is equal to θ which is of the same order as τ. (See p. 119.) We thus can write for investment in inventories:

$$J_{t+\theta} = e\,\frac{\Delta O_t}{\Delta t} \qquad (10.4)$$

It should be noticed that the coefficient e and the time lag θ are really averages. The relationship between changes in inventories and changes in output is very different for various commodities, and changes in inventories have no direct relation to changes in output of services (also included in O_t). If any stability in e can be expected at all it is only on the basis of a correlation between fluctuations of various components of the total output of the private sector, O.

It should be noticed that the phenomenon of accumulation of unsold goods is accounted for at least partly by the time lag θ in the equation (10.4). Indeed, when the volume of sales stops rising and begins to fall, inventories according to our formula will continue to rise for a time. This is not to deny, however, that in such circumstances the accumulation of unsold goods may continue on a larger scale than suggested by this formula. This deviation from the formula probably does not have a very serious bearing upon the overall theory of the trade cycle because this 'abnormal' accumulation of inventories is frequently liquidated in a relatively short time.

Determinants of investment

We obtained above the following formulae for investment in fixed capital, F, and for investment in inventories, J:

$$F_{t+\theta} = \frac{a}{1+c} S_t + b' \frac{\Delta P_t}{\Delta t} + d' \qquad (10.3)$$

$$J_{t+\theta} = e \frac{\Delta O_t}{\Delta t} \qquad (10.4)$$

Adding these two equations we obtain a formula for total investment, I:

$$I_{t+\theta} = \frac{a}{1+c} S_t + b' \frac{\Delta P_t}{\Delta t} + e \frac{\Delta O_t}{\Delta t} + d' \qquad (10.5)$$

S_t on the right-hand side depends on the *level* of economic activity at time t, while $\Delta P_t/\Delta t$ and $\Delta O_t/\Delta t$ depend on the *rate of change* in this level. The total investment thus depends, according to our theory, on both the level of economic activity and the rate of change in this level at some earlier time.

11. THE BUSINESS CYCLE

[(1943) 1954]

We shall assume in this chapter that both foreign trade and
the government budget are balanced and that workers do not
save. It was shown above in Chapter 8 that given this assumption the level of economic activity is determined by investment.
Moreover, it was shown in Chapter 10 that investment is determined, with a certain time lag, by the level of economic activity
and the rate of change in this level. It follows that investment
at a given time is determined by the level and rate of change in
the level of investment at some earlier time. It will be seen below
that this provides the basis for an analysis of the dynamic
economic process and in particular enables us to show that this
process involves cyclical fluctuations.

In addition to assuming a balanced foreign trade and budget
we shall also assume that the price index for deflating investment is identical with that for deflating the gross product of the
private sector. This assumption is not extravagant in view of
the rather small cyclical fluctuations in the ratio of prices of
investment and consumption goods (see p. 61). At the same
time a considerable simplification is achieved by it. Indeed, it
appeared necessary above to use different deflators in different
contexts for the same items. Thus, investment, savings and
profits were deflated in Chapters 7 and 8 by the same price
index as that used to deflate the gross product of the private
sector. But in Chapter 10 investment in fixed capital, savings
and profits were all deflated by the index of prices of investment
goods. However, now that the deflators have been assumed

identical, 'real' investment, savings and profits have one meaning only.

Let us now consider the equations which are relevant to our inquiry into the business cycle. From the assumption of a balanced foreign trade and budget it follows that saving is equal to investment:

$$S = I$$

Employing the same assumption, we may take from Chapter 7 (see p. 88) the equation relating profits after tax, P, with some time lag, to investment:

$$P_t = \frac{I_{t-\omega} + A}{1 - q} \tag{7.4'}$$

This equation is based: (*a*) on the equality between profits and investment plus capitalists' consumption; and (*b*) on the relation between capitalists' consumption and profits at some earlier time. (*A* is the stable part of capitalists' consumption and q is the coefficient of consumption out of an increment of profits.)

Furthermore, we derive from equations (8.2) and (8.1″) in Chapter 8 (see p. 102) the relation between gross product, O, and profits after tax, P:

$$O_t = \frac{P_t + B'}{1 - \alpha'} + E \tag{8.2'}$$

This equation reflects: (*a*) the factors determining the distribution of national income; (*b*) the system of profit taxes; and (*c*) the level of indirect taxes. (The constant B' and the coefficient α' reflect the 'distribution of income factors' and the system of profit taxes; the constant E stands for aggregate indirect taxes.)

Finally, Chapter 10 gives us the equation determining investment:

$$I_{t+\theta} = \frac{a}{1+c} S_t + b' \frac{\Delta P_t}{\Delta t} + e \frac{\Delta O_t}{\Delta t} + d'$$

This equation expresses: (*a*) the relation, with a time lag, between investment in fixed capital on the one hand and savings, the rate of change in profits and the rate of change in the stock of capital equipment on the other (the effect of the change in the stock of capital being reflected in the denominator of the coefficient $a/(1+c)$; and (b) the relation between investment in inventories and the rate of change in output.

From the latter equation and the assumed equality between savings and investment it follows:

$$I_{t+\theta} = \frac{a}{1+c} I_t + b' \frac{\Delta P_t}{\Delta t} + e \frac{\Delta O_t}{\Delta t} + d' \qquad (11.1)$$

THE EQUATION OF THE BUSINESS CYCLE

Equations (7.4'), (8.2') and (11.1) apply to the dynamic process in general. At the present stage, however, we intend to concentrate on the process of the business cycle as distinct from the process of long-run development. For this purpose we shall consider a system which is *not* subject to long-run development, i.e. a system which is static except for cyclical fluctuations. It can be shown† that the actual dynamic process can be analysed into (a) cyclical fluctuations, the pattern of which is the same as that in the static system described below; and (b) a smooth long-run trend.

To render our system 'static' we shall postulate that the parameters A, B' and E, which we have assumed throughout to be subject to long-run changes, are strictly constant. It follows directly then from equation (7.4') that:

$$\frac{\Delta P_t}{\Delta t} = \frac{1}{1-q} \frac{\Delta I_{t-\omega}}{\Delta t}$$

and from equation (8.2') that:

$$\frac{\Delta O_t}{\Delta t} = \frac{1}{1-\alpha'} \frac{\Delta P_t}{\Delta t}$$

---

† See M. Kalecki, *The Theory of Economic Dynamics* (London 1954), ch. 14.

or
$$\frac{\Delta O_t}{\Delta t} = \frac{1}{(1-q)(1-\alpha')} \frac{\Delta I_{t-\omega}}{\Delta t}$$

Both the rate of change in profits and the rate of change in output are here expressed in terms of the rate of change in investment (with a certain time lag). Substituting these expressions of $\Delta P/\Delta t$ and $\Delta O/\Delta t$ in equation (11.1) we obtain:

$$I_{t+\theta} = \frac{a}{1+c} I_t + \frac{b'}{1-q} \frac{\Delta I_{t-\omega}}{\Delta t} + \frac{e}{(1-q)(1-\alpha')} \frac{\Delta I_{t-\omega}}{\Delta t} + d'$$

or
$$I_{t+\theta} = \frac{a}{1+c} I_t + \frac{1}{1-q} \left(b' + \frac{e}{1-\alpha'} \right) \frac{\Delta I_{t-\omega}}{\Delta t} + d' \qquad (11.2)$$

Thus, investment at time $t+\theta$ is a function of investment at time t and of the rate of change in investment at time $t-\omega$. The first term on the right-hand side of the equation represents the influence on investment decisions of current savings (coefficient a) and also the negative effect of the increase in capital equipment (coefficient $1/(1+c)$). It should be remembered that $a/(1+c) < 1$. The second term represents the influence of the rate of change in profits (coefficient $b'/(1-q)$) and in output

$$\left(\text{coefficient } \frac{e}{(1-q)(1-\alpha')} \right)$$

In line with our tentative abstraction from long-run changes we assumed above that A, B' and E are strictly constant. The same must be assumed about d', but it will be seen that in addition the level of d' must conform to another condition if the system is to be 'static'. Indeed, such a system must be capable of being at rest at the level of investment equal to depreciation, δ. For this state of the system investment, I, is permanently stable at the level δ and $\Delta I/\Delta t$ is, of course, equal to zero. Equation (11.2) is thus reduced to:

$$\delta = \frac{a}{1+c} \delta + d' \qquad (11.3)$$

which is the condition d' must fulfil if the system is to be static in the sense that there is no long-run change. By subtracting equation (11.3) from equation (11.2) we obtain:

$$I_{t+\theta} - \delta = \frac{a}{1+c}(I_t - \delta) + \frac{1}{1-q}\left(b' + \frac{e}{1-\alpha'}\right)\frac{\Delta I_{t-\omega}}{\Delta t}$$

Let i denote $I - \delta$, the deviation of investment from depreciation. As δ is a constant† $\Delta i/\Delta t = \Delta I/\Delta t$ and we have:

$$i_{t+\theta} = \frac{a}{1+c}i_t + \frac{1}{1-q}\left(b' + \frac{e}{1-\alpha'}\right)\frac{\Delta i_{t-\omega}}{\Delta t} \qquad (11.4)$$

This is the equation which will serve as the basis of our analysis of the mechanism of the business cycle. For the sake of convenience we shall denote:

$$\frac{1}{1-q}\left(b' + \frac{e}{1-\alpha'}\right)$$

by μ. Equation (11.4) can then be written as:

$$i_{t+\theta} = \frac{a}{1+c}i_t + \mu\frac{\Delta i_{t-\omega}}{\Delta t} \qquad (11.4')$$

THE AUTOMATIC BUSINESS CYCLE

We shall now discuss the cyclical tendency inherent in equation (11.4'). In all of this discussion the assumption that the coefficient $a/(1+c)$ falls short of 1 is of crucial importance.

Let us imagine that we start from the position where $i_t = 0$, that is from the point A where investment is equal to depreciation (see Fig. 11.1). Let us imagine further that $(\Delta i_{t-\omega}/\Delta t) > 0$. This means that before A was reached investment was below but was increasing towards the level of depreciation. Now it is clear that $i_{t+\theta}$ is positive because the first component on the right-hand side of equation (11.4') $[a/(1+c)]i_t = 0$ and the second $\mu(\Delta i_{t-\omega}/\Delta t) > 0$. In other words, i has thus increased to point B above the depreciation level.

However, after i has become positive the question of its continuing rise, that is whether $i_{t+\theta}$ is higher than i_t, depends on the value of the coefficients $a/(1+c)$ and μ. Indeed, the first

† As a matter of fact depreciation fluctuates slightly in the course of the cycle, but δ may be conceived of as the average level of depreciation.

component of $i_{t+\theta}$, that is $[a/(1+c)]i_t$, is lower than i_t because we assumed that the coefficient $a/(1+c)$ was less than 1; and this tends to reduce $i_{t+\theta}$ below the level of i_t. On the other hand, the second component $\mu(\Delta i_{t-\omega}/\Delta t)$ is positive because i was rising before it reached the level of i_t and this tends to increase $i_{t+\theta}$ above the level of i_t. There are, therefore, two alternatives here: that the coefficients $a/(1+c)$ and μ are such that the rise of investment comes finally to a halt at a point C; or that the

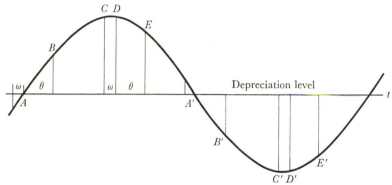

FIG. 11.1. Hypothetical time curve of investment. Illustration of the trend and cyclical components of gross investment.

rise continues until economic activity reaches a level where a further rise is prevented by scarcities in existing productive capacities or in available labour.

Let us consider the first alternative. After investment has come to a halt at C it cannot be maintained at this level, but must decline from D to E. Indeed, denoting the top level of i by i_{top} we have for point D:

$$i_t = i_{top}; \quad \frac{\Delta i_{t-\omega}}{\Delta t} = 0$$

Thus for $i_{t+\theta}$ at point E the component $\mu(\Delta i_{t-\omega}/\Delta t)$ is equal to zero and the component $[a/(1+c)]i_{top}$ is less than i_{top} because $a/(1+c) < 1$. Consequently, $i_{t+\theta}$ is less than i_{top} and investment declines from its highest level to that of point E.

Subsequently investment will move downwards, that is, $i_{t+\theta}$

will be lower than i_t for two reasons: the component $[a/(1+c)]i_t$ will be less than i_t and the component $\mu(\Delta i_{t-\omega}/\Delta t)$ will be negative. In this way i will finally fall to zero, i.e. investment will decline to the level of depreciation.

From this point on, the pattern of the boom will be repeated in reverse in the slump. After the depreciation level has been crossed downwards at A' the decline of investment will continue until it finally comes to a halt at C'. However, investment will not be maintained in this position but will increase from D' to E' and will again reach the depreciation level.

These fluctuations in investment will be accompanied by fluctuations in incomes, output and employment. The nature of the relationship between investment on the one hand and the aggregate real income and output of the private sector on the other are set forth in Chapter 8. (Cf. also pp. 135–7 of the present chapter.)

The above mechanism of the business cycle is based on two elements. (*a*) When investment reaches the depreciation level from below (at point A) it does not stop at this level but crosses it, moving upwards. This happens because the rise in investment and consequently the rise in profits and in aggregate output before the depreciation level is reached causes investment to be higher than that level in the subsequent period. Static equilibrium can come into existence only if investment is at the depreciation level and if in addition it has not changed its level in the recent past. The second condition is not fulfilled at A and this is the reason why the upward movement continues. When investment reaches the depreciation level from above (at A') the situation is analogous, i.e. investment does not stop but crosses the depreciation level moving downwards.

(*b*) When the upward movement of investment comes to a halt it does not stay at this level, but starts to decline. This happens because the coefficient $a/(1+c)$ is less than 1, which reflects the negative influence upon investment of the increasing capital equipment ($c > 0$) and possibly also the factor of incomplete reinvestment of saving (if $a < 1$). If there were a full reinvestment of saving (i.e. $a = 1$) and if the accumulation of capital equipment could be disregarded (i.e. if c were negligible) the system would be maintained at its top level. But, in fact, the accumulation of capital equipment, which with a stable level of economic activity makes for a falling rate of profit, does have a tangible adverse effect on investment (i.e. c is not negligible). Moreover, the reinvestment of savings may be incomplete (i.e. $a < 1$).† As a result, investment declines and thus the slump is started.‡

The position at the bottom of the slump is analogous to that at the top of the boom. While the rate of profit is falling at the top of the boom because of additions to the stock of capital equipment, it is rising at the bottom of the slump because depreciation of capital equipment is not being made good.§

But it may be questioned whether this situation is symmetrical with that at the top of the boom. It may indeed be claimed that the effect of capital destruction upon investment decisions during the slump is much weaker than that of capital accumulation in the boom because the equipment 'destroyed' in the slump is frequently idle in any case. As a result, slumps might be very long. This possibility is, in fact, not excluded in the static system which we consider in this chapter.|| But it should be observed that the situation is different in an economy enjoying long-run growth. It can be shown that in such an economy the business cycle as described above is superimposed upon the smooth long-run trend.¶

† The importance of the 'incomplete reinvestment' factor for the explanation of the turning point in the boom was emphasized for the first time by the late E. Rothbarth in a lecture to the Economic Society of the London School of Economics in 1939.

‡ This analysis shows clearly that the assumption $a/(1+c) < 1$ is a necessary condition for the existence of the business cycle (cf. p. 120).

§ If $a < 1$ this will be an additional factor in the recovery of investment from the bottom of the slump. The condition $a < 1$ means in this context that fixed capital investment decisions fall in the slump less than savings, if we abstract from the influence of the rate of change in profits and in capital equipment.

|| In such a case c is smaller, and thus $a/(1+c)$ is larger, in the depression than in the boom.

¶ In Fig. 18, p. 147, of *Theory of Economic Dynamics*, reproduced overleaf, we see that at point D', corresponding to the bottom of the slump, the level of economic

THE 'CEILING' AND THE 'FLOOR'

The above considerations were based on the assumption that the coefficients of $a/(1+c)$ and μ are such as to cause an automatic halt to the rise of investment in the boom and to its fall in the slump. In the alternative case the rise of investment in the boom will not come to a halt until hampered by shortages of equipment or labour. When this position is reached, unfilled orders will pile up rapidly while deliveries will lag behind requirements. This will result in stopping the rise or even in producing a fall of investment in inventories. Investment in fixed capital may be similarly affected by shortages in this sector. The period of execution of investment orders will lengthen and the rise of investment in fixed capital will have to taper off.

After the rise in the rate of investment has come to a halt and the level of economic activity has been maintained for some time at this 'ceiling', the mechanism of the business cycle begins to operate. Investment starts falling, as in the case considered above, as a result of increases in the stock of capital equipment

activity is actually increasing at the rate of the long-run growth, while the expansion of capital equipment falls short of this rate so that the rate of profit is increasing.

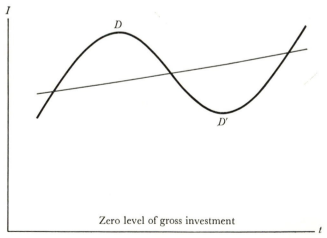

Illustration of the trend and cyclical components of gross investment.

and possibly also because of an incomplete reinvestment of savings (which factors make $a/[1+c] < 1$). Having started in this fashion, the slump continues in the same way as the 'automatic' business cycle.

The question arises whether there is a 'floor' to the slump in the same sense that there is a 'ceiling' to the boom. Such a 'floor' certainly exists in the case of investment in fixed capital since its gross value cannot fall below zero. However, there is no analogous limit to disinvestment in inventories. Thus, when gross investment in fixed capital reaches the zero level, the slump may be slowed down but not halted since disinvestment in inventories may gather momentum. If, however, the slump does come to a halt the process of recovery is much like that described in the preceding section.

EXPLOSIVE AND DAMPED FLUCTUATIONS

Let us turn back to the case of the automatic business cycle. It appears that the cyclical fluctuations inherent in the equation

$$i_{t+\theta} = \frac{a}{1+c} i_t + \mu \frac{\Delta i_{t-\omega}}{\Delta t} \qquad (11.4')$$

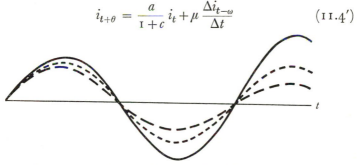

FIG. 11.2. Stable, damped, and explosive fluctuations.

may be stable, explosive, or damped (see Fig. 11.2) depending on the value of the coefficients, $a/(1+c)$ and μ, and the time-lags θ and ω. Given a certain set of these values the amplitude of fluctuations is constant. But if the coefficient μ is increased while $a/(1+c)$, θ and ω remain unchanged, the fluctuations become explosive; and if μ is reduced they become damped.

Let us first consider the case of explosive fluctuations. It is clear that, due to the increasing amplitude of the fluctuations, investment, during the boom phase, must sooner or later strike the 'ceiling'. After this, as shown above, there follows a slump, the recovery from which brings investment back again to the level of the 'ceiling', and so on. (See Fig. 11.3) The bottom of the slump is maintained at the same level because the course of the downswing is fully determined, according to equation (11.4′) by the level i at the top of the boom, the coefficients $a/(1+c)$ and μ, and the time lags θ and ω.

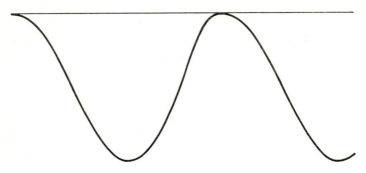

FIG. 11.3. Explosive fluctuations with a 'ceiling'.

In the case of damped fluctuations the amplitude will continuously decline, so that it might appear in this case that the cycle would dwindle into insignificance. This, however, is not correct, for the following reason. The relations between investment, profits and output, on which equation (11.4′) is based, are 'stochastic', i.e. subject to random disturbances. (The deviations of the actual from the calculated values in the statistical illustrations given above may be interpreted as such disturbances.) Thus equation (11.4′) really should be written:

$$i_{t+\theta} = \frac{a}{1+c} i_t + \mu \frac{\Delta i_{t-\omega}}{\Delta t} + \epsilon \qquad (11.4'')$$

where ϵ is a random disturbance. Now it appears that the effect of 'erratic shocks', ϵ, in equation (11.4″) counteracts the damping inherent in the basic mechanism. As a result some sort of semi-regular cyclical movement is generated, the amplitude of which is determined by the magnitude and pattern of shocks, ϵ, and by the parameters of equation (11.4').†

This result is of considerable importance. It shows the possibility of cyclical fluctuations which do not touch the 'ceiling' and thus helps to explain the fact that such is frequently the pattern of actual fluctuations. A serious difficulty arises, however, in the application of the theory. The experiments made seem to suggest that if the damping is not weak the resulting cycle is very irregular and its amplitude is of the order of magnitude of the shocks. Since there is no reasonable basis for the assumption that the inter-relations between investment, profits and output should necessarily be such as to produce a weak damping, the value of the theory becomes questionable. This difficulty is dealt with in Chapter 13 of my *Theory of Economic Dynamics*, where it is shown that if certain justifiable assumptions are made about the character of the shocks, a fairly regular cycle with a relatively large amplitude emerges even when the damping is substantial.

THE BUSINESS CYCLE AND UTILIZATION OF RESOURCES

It has already been stated above (see p. 130) that fluctuations in investment will cause corresponding fluctuations in economic activity as a whole. Indeed, aggregate output is related to investment through equations (7.4') and (8.2'). Also, it has been stated that aggregate output and consumption show smaller relative fluctuations than investment (see p. 97).

We have, however, not yet examined the problem of fluctuations in the utilization of capital equipment. We shall see below that the volume of fixed capital fluctuates relatively little in the

† It also appears that if the basic mechanism tends to produce fluctuations of a constant amplitude erratic shocks cause the cycle to become explosive. Consequently, sooner or later the 'ceiling' is reached and from then on the amplitude does not change.

course of the cycle so that fluctuations in output reflect mainly changes in the degree of utilization of equipment.

This can be shown by the following example which is relevant to developed capitalist economies. We assume that the depreciation level is 5 per cent per annum of the average volume of fixed capital equipment and that gross investment in fixed capital fluctuates between 7·5 per cent and 2·5 per cent of this volume. Thus, investment falls in the slump to one-third of the boom level. We assume, moreover, that at the top of the boom gross investment in fixed capital constitutes 20 per cent of the aggregate output (i.e. the gross product of the private sector). Thus, since investment falls from the top of the boom to the bottom of the slump by two-thirds, the drop in investment amounts to about 13 per cent of the boom aggregate output. We further assume that the change in output, ΔO, is equal to 2·5 times the change in investment, ΔI.[†] It follows that the fall in output from the top of the boom to the bottom of the slump is equal to 2·5 times 13 per cent, that is, 33 per cent of the boom output level. Thus, output falls by about one-third from the top of the boom to the bottom of the slump. It will easily be seen that the amplitude of fluctuations is about 20 per cent of the average level.[‡]

Let us now calculate the amplitude of fluctuations of the stock of capital equipment. The largest addition of fixed capital takes place in the period MN (see Fig. 11.4) because this is the stretch of time in which gross investment in fixed capital is over the depreciation level.

Now, the highest level of gross investment in the boom has been assumed to be 7·5 per cent of the average volume of the capital equipment and, therefore, with depreciation equal to 5 per cent the highest net investment is 2·5 per cent.[§] We

[†] According to p. 101 a change in investment of ΔI in the United States in the period 1929–40 was accompanied by a change in real income of the private sector of 2·72 ΔI.

[‡] $\frac{1}{2} \times \frac{1}{3} : (1 - \frac{1}{2} \cdot \frac{1}{3}) = \frac{1}{5}$.

[§] Maximum investment in fixed capital is approximately equal to maximum total investment; indeed, investment in inventories at the top of the boom is small because of the levelling off of the aggregate output.

assume the length of the cycle to be 10 years and thus the length of the period *MN* is 5 years. If throughout that period investment in fixed capital were at the highest level, the total addition to the volume of capital equipment would be 12·5 per cent of its average level. In fact, however, as may be seen from Fig. 11.4, this addition will only be around two-thirds of 12·5 per cent or 8 per cent. Consequently, the amplitude of fluctuations in the stock of fixed capital in relation to its average level will be around 4 per cent as compared with 20 per cent for output.

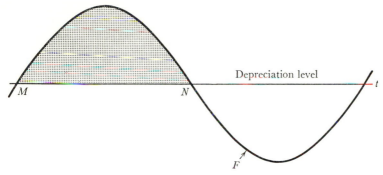

FIG. 11.4. The effect of fluctuations in investment in fixed capital, *F*, upon the stock of capital equipment.

It is thus clear that fluctuations in the degree of utilization of equipment are of similar order as those in aggregate output. A considerable proportion of capital equipment lies idle in the slump. Even on the average the degree of utilization throughout the business cycle will be substantially below the maximum reached during the boom. Fluctuations in the utilization of available labour parallel those in the utilization of equipment. Not only is there mass unemployment in the slump, but average employment throughout the cycle is considerably below the peak reached in the boom. The reserve of capital equipment and the reserve army of unemployed are typical features of capitalist economy at least throughout a considerable part of the cycle.

PART III

12. POLITICAL ASPECTS OF FULL EMPLOYMENT

[1943]

The maintenance of full employment through government spending financed by loans has been widely discussed in recent years. This discussion, however, has concentrated on the purely economic aspects of the problem without paying due consideration to political realities. The assumption that a Government will maintain full employment in a capitalist economy if it only knows how to do it is fallacious. In this connection the misgivings of big business about maintenance of full employment by Government spending are of paramount importance. This attitude was shown clearly in the great depression in the thirties, when big business opposed consistently experiments for increasing employment by Government spending in all countries, except Nazi Germany. The attitude is not easy to explain. Clearly higher output and employment benefits not only workers, but businessmen as well, because their profits rise. And the policy of full employment based on loan financed Government spending does not encroach upon profits because it does not involve any additional taxation. The businessmen in the slump are longing for a boom; why do not they accept gladly the 'synthetic' boom which the Government is able to offer them? It is this difficult and fascinating question with which we intend to deal in this article.

Political aspects

1. The reasons for the opposition of the 'industrial leaders' to full employment achieved by Government spending may be subdivided into three categories: (i) the dislike of Government interference in the problem of employment as such; (ii) the dislike of the direction of Government spending (public investment and subsidising consumption); (iii) dislike of the social and political changes resulting from the *maintenance* of full employment. We shall examine each of these three categories of objections to the Government expansion policy in detail.

2. We shall deal first with the reluctance of the 'captains of industry' to accept Government intervention in the matter of employment. Every widening of State activity is looked upon by 'business' with suspicion, but the creation of employment by Government spending has a special aspect which makes the opposition particularly intense. Under a *laisser-faire* system the level of employment depends to a great extent on the so-called state of confidence. If this deteriorates, private investment declines, which results in a fall of output and employment (both directly and through the secondary effect of the fall in incomes upon consumption and investment). This gives to the capitalists a powerful indirect control over Government policy: everything which may shake the state of confidence must be carefully avoided because it would cause an economic crisis. But once the Government learns the trick of increasing employment by its own purchases, this powerful controlling device loses its effectiveness. Hence budget deficits necessary to carry out Government intervention must be regarded as perilous. The social function of the doctrine of 'sound finance' is to make the level of employment dependent on the 'state of confidence'.

3. The dislike of the business leaders of a Government spending policy grows even more acute when they come to consider the objects on which the money would be spent: public investment and subsidising mass consumption.

The economic principles of Government intervention require

that public investment should be confined to objects which do not compete with the equipment of private business, e.g. hospitals, schools, highways, etc. Otherwise the profitability of private investment might be impaired and the positive effect of public investment upon employment offset by the negative effect of the decline in private investment. This conception suits the business men very well. But the scope of public investment of this type is rather narrow, and there is a danger that the Government, in pursuing this policy, may eventually be tempted to nationalise transport or public utilities so as to gain a new sphere in which to carry out investment.†

One might therefore expect business leaders and their experts to be more in favour of subsidising mass consumption (by means of family allowances, subsidies to keep down the prices of necessities, etc.) than of public investment; for by subsidising consumption the Government would not be embarking on any sort of 'enterprise'. In practice, however, this is not the case. Indeed, subsidising mass consumption is much more violently opposed by these 'experts' than public investment. For here a 'moral' principle of the highest importance is at stake. The fundamentals of capitalist ethics require that 'You shall earn your bread in sweat'—unless you happen to have private means.

4. We have considered the political reasons for the opposition against the policy of creating employment by Government spending. But even if this opposition were overcome—as it may well be under the pressure of the masses—the *maintenance* of full employment would cause social and political changes which would give a new impetus to the opposition of the business leaders. Indeed, under a regime of permanent full employment, 'the sack' would cease to play its role as a disciplinary measure. The social position of the boss would be undermined and the

† It should be noticed here that investment in a nationalised industry can contribute to the solution of the problem of unemployment only if it is undertaken on principles different from these of private enterprise. The Government may have to be satisfied with a lower net rate of return than private enterprise and must deliberately time its investment so as to mitigate slumps.

self assurance and class consciousness of the working class would grow. Strikes for wage increases and improvements in conditions of work would create political tension. It is true that profits would be higher under a regime of full employment than they are on the average under *laisser-faire*; and even the rise in wage rates resulting from the stronger bargaining power of the workers is less likely to reduce profits than to increase prices, and thus affects adversely only the rentier interests. But 'discipline in the factories' and 'political stability' are more appreciated by the business leaders than profits. Their class instinct tells them that lasting full employment is unsound from their point of view and that unemployment is an integral part of the normal capitalist system.

II

1. One of the important functions of fascism, as typified by the Nazi system, was to remove the capitalist objections to full employment.

The dislike of Government spending policy as such is overcome under fascism by the fact that the State machinery is under the direct control of a partnership of big business with fascist upstarts. The necessity for the myth of 'sound finance' which served to prevent the Government from offsetting a confidence crisis by spending, is removed. In a democracy one does not know what the next Government will be like. Under fascism there is no next Government.

The dislike of Government spending, whether on public investment or consumption, is overcome by concentrating Government expenditure on armaments. Finally, 'discipline in the factories' and 'political stability' under full employment are maintained by the 'new order', which ranges from the suppression of the trade unions to the concentration camp. Political pressure replaces the economic pressure of unemployment.

2. The fact that armaments are the backbone of the policy of fascist full employment has a profound influence upon its economic character.

Large-scale armaments are inseparable from the expansion of the armed forces and the preparation of plans for a war of conquest. They also induce competitive rearmament of other countries. This causes the main aim of the spending to shift gradually from full employment to securing the maximum effect of rearmament. The resulting scarcity of resources leads to the curtailment of consumption as compared with what it could have been under full employment.

The fascist system starts from the overcoming of unemployment, develops into an 'armament economy' of scarcity, and ends inevitably in war.

III

1. What will be the practical outcome of the opposition to 'full employment by Government spending' in a capitalist democracy? We shall try to answer this question on the basis of the analysis of the reasons for this opposition given in section 1 (pp. 139–40). We argued that we may expect the opposition of the 'leaders of industry' on three planes: (i) the opposition on principle against Government spending based on a budget deficit; (ii) the opposition against this spending being directed either towards public investment—which may foreshadow the intrusion of the state into the new spheres of economic activity—or towards subsidising mass consumption; (iii) the opposition against *maintaining* full employment and not merely preventing deep and prolonged slumps.

Now, it must be recognised that the stage in which the 'business leaders' could afford to be opposed to *any* kind of Government interventions to alleviate a slump is rather a matter of the past. The necessity that 'something must be done in the slump' is agreed to; but the conflict continues, firstly, as to what should be the direction of Government intervention in the slump, and secondly, as to whether it should be used merely to alleviate slumps or to secure permanent full employment.

2. In the current discussions of these problems there emerges time and again the conception of counteracting the slump by

stimulating *private* investment. This may be done by lowering the rate of interest, by the reduction of income tax, or by subsidising private investment directly in this or another form. That such a scheme should be attractive to 'business' is not surprising. The businessman remains the medium through which the intervention is conducted. If he does not feel confidence in the political situation he will not be bribed into investment. And the intervention does not involve the Government either in 'playing with' (public) investment or 'wasting money' on subsidising consumption.

It may be shown, however, that the stimulation of private investment does not provide an adequate method for preventing mass unemployment. There are two alternatives to be considered here: (*a*) The rate of interest or income tax—or both—is reduced sharply in the slump and increased in the boom. In this case both the period and the amplitude of the business cycle will be reduced, but employment not only in the slump but even in the boom may be far from full, i.e. the average unemployment may be considerable, although its fluctuations will be less marked; (*b*) The rate of interest or income tax is reduced in a slump but *not* increased in the subsequent boom. In this case the boom will last longer but it must end in a new slump: one reduction in the rate of interest or income tax does not, of course, eliminate the forces which cause cyclical fluctuations in a capitalist economy. In the new slump it will be necessary to reduce the rate of interest or income tax again and so on. Thus in not too remote a time the rate of interest would have to be negative and income tax would have to be replaced by an income subsidy. The same would arise if it were attempted to *maintain* full employment by stimulating private investment: the rate of interest and income tax would have to be reduced continuously.

In addition to this fundamental weakness of combating unemployment by stimulating private investment, there is a practical difficulty. The reaction of businessmen to the measures described is uncertain. If the down-swing is sharp they may take a very pessimistic view of the future, and the reduction of the rate of interest or income tax may then for a long time have little or no effect upon investment, and thus upon the level of output and employment.

3. Even those who advocate stimulating private investment to counteract the slump frequently do not rely on it exclusively but envisage that it should be associated with public investment. It looks at present as if 'business leaders' and their experts—at least part of them—would tend to accept as a *pis aller* public expenditure financed by borrowing as a means of alleviating slumps. They seem, however, still to be consistently opposed to creating employment by subsidising consumption and to *maintaining* full employment.

This state of affairs is perhaps symptomatic of the future economic regime of capitalist democracies. In the slump, either under the pressure of the masses, or even without it, public investment financed by borrowing will be undertaken to prevent large-scale unemployment. But if attempts are made to apply this method in order to maintain the high level of employment reached in the subsequent boom a strong opposition of 'business leaders' is likely to be encountered. As has already been argued, lasting full employment is not at all to their liking. The workers would 'get out of hand' and the 'captains of industry' would be anxious to 'teach them a lesson'. Moreover, the price increase in the up-swing is to the disadvantage of small and big *rentiers* and makes them 'boom tired'.

In this situation a powerful block is likely to be formed between big business and the *rentier* interests, and they would probably find more than one economist to declare that the situation was manifestly unsound. The pressure of all these forces, and in particular of big business would most probably induce the Government to return to the orthodox policy of cutting down the budget deficit. A slump would follow in which Government spending policy would come again into its own.

This pattern of a 'political business cycle' is not entirely conjectural; something very much like that happened in the U.S.A. in 1937–8. The breakdown of the boom in the second half of 1937 was actually due to the drastic reduction of the budget deficit. On the other hand, in the acute slump that followed, the Government promptly reverted to a spending policy.

13. THE PROBLEM OF
EFFECTIVE DEMAND WITH
TUGAN-BARANOVSKI AND
ROSA LUXEMBURG

[1967]

In the discussions about the market for the national product in terms of the Marxian schemes of reproduction, the positions taken by Tugan-Baranovski and Rosa Luxemburg are on the two opposite poles. Tugan-Baranovski denies altogether that the problem of markets may constitute an obstacle to the development of capitalism which thus depends entirely on the increase in productive capacity. Rosa Luxemburg on the contrary considers expanded reproduction in a closed capitalist system impossible, attributing all its development to the possibility of selling its wares in the markets external to it, i.e. in the non-capitalist sector of the world economy.

It is most interesting that both authors commit important errors in their arguments and that nevertheless their theories give a correct picture of some essentials of capitalist economy. Tugan-Baranovski rightly stresses the 'antagonistic character' of the capitalist regime, as a result of which the production of consumer goods is not its final aim and the demand for them is not the motive force of its development. Similarly, although the Rosa Luxemburg's theory that the development of capitalism depends solely on the 'external markets' is not correct, they are still an important part in its dynamics.

The two theories find something like a point of intersection in the present day—especially U.S.—capitalism where a decisive role is played by a market created by the government for armament production.

I

The theory of Tugan-Baranovski is in fact very simple: the author maintains that with 'appropriate proportions' of use made of national product the problem of effective demand does not arise. This argument, illustrated numerically by means of Marxian schemes of reproduction, is in fact tantamount to the statement that at any level of consumption of workers and capitalists the national product may be sold provided investment is sufficiently large. These are the 'proportions' between consumption and investment, which must be established in order that the total production should be purchased. A distortion of this proportion leads to crises in the course of which the deviation from it is being corrected. Thus the fundamental idea of Tugan rests on an error that what *may* happen is actually happening, because he does not show at all why capitalists in the long-run are to invest to the extent which is necessary to contribute to full utilization of productive equipment.

Tugan stresses the point that his theory will be right even in the most adverse conditions of actual curtailment of consumption of the workers and stability of that of capitalists. Obviously on paper even this may be offset by a sufficiently high level of investment. The author, by the way, does not anticipate the criticism that capitalists may be unwilling to use the surplus value by investing so much. He rather answers a critic of a different type who would consider absurd investment the purpose of which is production of investment goods rather than that of consumer goods. After having 'fixed' his critic in this way Tugan gives a perfectly sensible answer.

The capitalist system is not a 'harmonious' regime, whose purpose is the satisfaction of the needs of its citizens but an 'antagonistic' regime which is to secure profits for capitalists. As a result there is nothing absurd in basing the development of the system on expansion of a production of 'coal and steel' which serves to develop the production of these commodities. The production of 'coal and steel' is as justified as production of bread if it is profitable. Consumption is the final aim and proof of a 'harmonious' but not of an 'antagonistic' regime.

It is this part of the argument of Tugan-Baranovski that I consider his lasting contribution to the analysis of functioning of capitalism in its various phases. It is worth noticing that the theory of Tugan is despite his 'optimism' deeply anticapitalistic: it is just the absurdity of capitalism that makes its development immune against the problem of finding markets for its products.

III

Let us go back, however, to our critique of the theory of Tugan-Baranovski (which is equivalent to the statement of Rosa Luxemburg on the subject of this theory). Tugan considers the *possible* use of the national product created by full utilization of the productive forces as the actual fact—in any case if we disregard the business cycles. The following problem arises here: the approach is certainly faulty, from which however does not follow that Tugan's theory is wrong, but merely completely unfounded. Perhaps after all the problem of the markets does not really constitute an obstacle to expanded reproduction of a capitalist economy. In order to give a complete answer to this query it is necessary to construct a theory of investment decisions such that it would cover all the aspects of dynamics of capitalist economy and not only those relevant to the business cycle. This is not the place however, to develop such a theory which I always considered to be the central problem of the political economy of capitalism. Here I shall try to show that expanded reproduction—even in conditions much more favourable than were on purpose assumed by Tugan-Baranovski—is by no means obvious and that it requires a certain supporting factor, for instance, dependent on innovations (and thus not necessarily Rosa Luxemburg's 'external markets').

Imagine the process of accumulation of capital, say 4 per cent per annum. Let us assume that at the start the capital equipment and labour are fully utilised. Let the depreciation amount to 3 per cent per annum so that gross investment is equal to 7 per cent of capital. Let us also assume a constant share of gross profits (including depreciation) in the gross national product, and constant proportions in the distribution of gross profits between gross accumulation and capitalists' consumption. Thus gross accumulation bears a constant relation to the national income. The process of accumulation consists in the expansion of productive equipment at 4 per cent per annum due to investment, and since gross accumulation bears a constant relation (7 per cent) to capital, gross accumulation also expands 4 per cent per annum. Given the constant share of gross accumulation in national income, income would also grow at the 4 per cent per annum rate. Thus full utilisation of equipment continues and the problem of effective demand does not seem to arise.

All right, but why should capitalists continue to invest at a level of 7 per cent of capital? Simply because the process has been going for some time, this investment has been 'justified' and the capitalists do not anticipate any difficulties in selling their products with reproduction expanding 4 per cent per annum, and therefore they do not hesitate to continue their game.

Let us, however, consider a case when—for instance, as a result of a change in the social structure of the capitalist class—capitalists are prepared to invest only 6 per cent of the capital per annum (without changing the relative share of their consumption in gross profits). The problem of effective demand makes then immediately its appearance. The ratio of investment to the stock of capital falls by $\frac{1}{7}$, i.e. by about 14 per cent. There arises thus the problem of overproduction: because of the constancy of relation between accumulated and consumed part of profits the latter will also fall by 14 per cent in relation to capital; through reduction of employment in investment goods industries and in industries producing consumption goods for capitalists there will be also a reduction of demand for wage goods and reduction of employment in those industries—until working class income also falls by 14 per cent in relation to capital so that the proportion between profits and wages be maintained as assumed. This general situation of overproduction affects in turn adversely the investment decisions of capitalists. Now they are not willing to invest even 6 per cent of capital, contributing thus to further deterioration of the situation.

Yes, somebody may say, this is a typical crisis which will be followed by a period of prosperity and these fluctuations will just occur around the process of expanded reproduction described initially. There is, however, nothing to substantiate this argument. After a breakdown of the moving equilibrium no trace of the 4 or 3 per cent annual long-run increase was left in the economy. The economy may as well settle to a state of simple reproduction with cyclical fluctuations around it.

IV

We have moved one step forward: we have shown that the development of capitalism which does not encounter the problem of effective demand, even if it is possible, is unstable. However, a process of an unstable equilibrium ceases to exist if it is not supported by some stabilizing force. In relation to our problem it may be said that an expanded reproduction will take place if there exist factors that simply do not permit the system to remain in the state of simple reproduction (or stationary state): the initial state of simple reproduction leads to a level of gross investment exceeding depreciation.

Such a factor may be first and foremost the influence of technological innovations, discovery of new sources of raw materials and the like which opens before the capitalists new perspectives. The technical progress appears in this approach not merely as depreciating old plant, which leads to their replacement by new ones; it is also a stimulus for investment over and above that level resulting from the fact that capitalists investing 'today' think to have an advantage over those having invested 'yesterday' because of technical novelties that have reached them.

The above should not be construed in the sense that such a possibility of expanded reproduction—without 'external markets'—is tantamount to the elimination of influence of inadequate effective demand. Indeed the rate of expanded reproduction resulting from this factor is by no means necessarily adequate to secure the full utilisation of equipment or even to keep the degree of this utilization at a constant level. Innovations break the impasse of a simple reproduction only to some extent and they do not warrant the utilization of resources in the sense of Tugan-Baranovski.

From the last two sections it follows in any case: (*a*) as a result of the problem of effective demand, expanded reproduction is not a natural and obvious state of the capitalist system; (*b*) nevertheless such reproduction is not necessarily a result of 'external markets'. Thus although these sections are meant primarily as a criticism of the theory of Tugan-Baranovski they constitute at the same time a starting point for a discussion of views of Rosa Luxemburg with which we shall deal subsequently.

v

Rosa Luxemburg considers expanded reproduction in the long run without existence of 'external markets' to be not only far from obvious but outright impossible. It should be noticed that she argues this point as naïvely as does Tugan-Baranovski showing the irrelevance of the problem of effective demand for the development of capitalism. In her consideration of the taking of investment decisions by capitalists she somehow implies that they are being taken by the capitalist class as a whole. And this class is frustrated by the knowledge that there is no final market for the surplus of goods corresponding to accumulation: so why invest?

Now capitalists do many things as a class but they certainly do not invest as a class. And if that *were* the case they might do it just in the way prescribed by Tugan-Baranovski. But despite this error in her argument, it is valuable in being imbued by the spirit of scepticism with regard to the market for the surplus of goods corresponding to the accumulation. Even though following a different line of thought, we also have come to the conclusion that expanded reproduction is by no means a 'natural' phenomenon, and we tried to find the source of expanded reproduction—which is, though, by no means equivalent to permanent full utilization of equipment—in certain aspects of technical progress.

Rosa Luxemburg, as we mentioned time and again above, sees the possibility of finding the market for surplus goods merely *outside* the world capitalist system. She does not mean here underdeveloped countries only but also the non-capitalist sectors of developed economies, e.g. peasant agriculture. Only the 'exports' from the capitalist system are the mainspring of development. Hence her pessimistic view of the future of capitalism: by undermining the non-capitalist production and gradually pervading all the world, capitalism eliminates at the same time the possibility of its further development.

To the quantitative overestimate of the role of 'external markets' Rosa Luxemburg contributes a fundamental mistake which she perpetrates in the analysis of the impact of these markets on development of capitalism. She considers—in any case in the main current of her argument—that the market for the surplus is created to the extent of *total* exports to the non-capitalist sector and not only to the extent of the *excess* of exports over imports.

It is easy to show, however, that this approach of Rosa Luxemburg's is erroneous: the imported goods absorb purchasing power just like those home-produced, and thus to the extent that exports are offset by imports they do not contribute to the expansion of the markets for national product. Or to approach it from a different angle, imports, like wages, are costs, and the part of disposal of profits is, alongside capitalists' consumption and investment, solely the export surplus. And in order that this should be possible export of capital is necessary. Only to the extent to which the capitalist system lends to the non-capitalist world (or the latter sells its assets) is it possible to place abroad the surplus of goods unsold at home. Only in this way do 'the external markets' solve the contradictions of the world capitalist system.

Obviously the net 'external markets' as well played their role in development of capitalism, but a much more modest one than would have been the case if really *all* the exports to the non-capitalist world contributed to the absorption of surpluses corresponding to accumulation.

VI

One of the most interesting elements of the theory of Rosa Luxemburg is taking into consideration in her 'external markets', alongside those mentioned above, also the market created by government purchases and in particular armament orders. She consistently makes, by the way, the mistake of treating the *whole* of government expenditure, for instance on armaments, without paying due consideration to its financing, as absorbing the surplus.

If, however, this expenditure is covered by taxes burdening the working class they have no effect upon the absorption of national product because the new 'armaments markets' are offset by an equal curtailment of workers' consumption.

If armaments are financed by issue of government securities, then the surplus of goods is sold by capitalists in exchange for the money obtained in turn by the government through sale of their bills and bonds to the financial capitalists. The capitalists —taken as a whole—thus grant the government a credit with which to buy their surplus goods. Also here capital is being 'exported' to the 'foreign market' created by the government (this operation may be transacted through the banking system—

the government sells bills to the latter using the amounts obtained to purchase armaments; while in the banking system there is an equal increase in deposits representing the accumulation corresponding to the armament production. As a result the capitalists grant to the government credits through the medium of the banking system.

Finally even when the armament expenditure of the government is covered by the tax on profits it also constitutes a way of absorbing to this extent accumulation but in a different way from the case of financing this expenditure by internal credits. Imagine that profits accumulated by capitalists as a whole as a result of armament orders are taken away by taxation rather than in exchange for government securities.

The profits do not increase then as a result of new armament orders but the surplus is nevertheless absorbed by its expropriation by the government. The difference from the case considered previously consists in the fact that while there the capitalists granted to the government credits, they pay taxes in the case presently considered.

Thus Rosa Luxemburg rightly saw in the armament orders an 'external market' which can absorb a part of accumulation —but she should have excluded from this type of 'external markets' the case where armaments are financed by taxation of the workers.

It should be added still that Rosa Luxemburg does not treat the 'external markets' created by the government as a problem of first rate importance. Thus while predicting the general crisis of capitalism caused by the exhaustion of non-capitalist markets, she does not anticipate the possibility of counteracting that crisis by the 'external market' of government purchases.

VII

It follows from the above what was said at the outset of this paper that theories both of Tugan-Baranovski and Rosa Luxemburg find in a sense their confirmation in contemporary, in particular American, capitalism. While perpetrating grave mistakes in their arguments the authors show a striking perspicacity in the evaluation of certain basic elements of late stage capitalism.

The 'external markets' in the broad sense of Rosa Luxemburg in the form of armament orders and ancillary expenditure —insofar as they are financed by loans and taxation of capitalists—play today a leading role in the functioning of modern capitalism. It is true that Rosa Luxemburg did not anticipate the enormous role of this type of 'external market' in the absorption of accumulation. But one way or another she maintained that capitalism is saved by 'external markets'. In her time it was no doubt exaggerated but it has proved right today.

As for Tugan-Baranovski, contemporary capitalism indeed put into focus his view of the paradoxical and absurd character of 'antagonistic systems' whose main task is not catering to human needs. In his vision of future capitalism, machines were to produce machines for production of machines. But making the high level of employment and workers' consumption dependent on production of the means of destruction is even more absurd.

Both, despite slips in their arguments contributed to the understanding of the queer and perverse world in which we are living.

14. CLASS STRUGGLE
AND DISTRIBUTION OF
NATIONAL INCOME

[1971]

1. Until fairly recently it was generally accepted that if wages are raised profits decline *pro tanto*. Even though in the analysis of other phenomena Say's law was not adhered to, at least not strictly, in this case the preservation of purchasing power was not put to doubt. And the analysis of increase or reduction in wage rates dealt with the physical consequences of this absolute shift from profits to wages or *vice versa*. In the case of the rise in wage rates, the reconstruction of capital equipment in line with the higher spending on wage goods and lower outlays on investment and capitalists' consumption was emphasized; as well as the tendency to higher unemployment as a result of substitution of capital for labour that has become more expensive.

Although even to-day quite a number of economists would argue in this fashion the fallacy of this approach is fairly widely recognized, even though it may be countered by various economists in a somewhat different way. My counterargument runs as follows. I assume in it a closed economic system and a proportional rise in all wage rates.

Suppose that in a short period of time the annual wage bill increased as a result of raising wage rates by ΔW. We may assume realistically that workers spend all their incomes and that they spend them immediately. As contrasted with this, it may be assumed that the volume of investment and capitalists' consumption are determined by decisions taken prior to the

156

short period considered and are not affected by the wage rise during that period.

If we now subdivide the economy into three departments, producing investment goods (I), consumption goods for capitalists (II) and wage goods (III)—including into each of them the respective intermediate products—it follows that employment in the first two departments is not affected by the rise in wages. Thus denoting the wage bills in these departments measured in 'old' wage rates by W_1 and W_2 and the fraction by which wages are raised by α we obtain for the increment of the aggregate wages in Departments I and II $\alpha(W_1 + W_2)$. The profits in these two departments decline *pro tanto* (provided prices of their products have not risen which in any case is assumed in the argument based on 'preservation of purchasing power').

The position in Department III, however, is quite different because of immediate spending of the additional proceeds of the workers due to the wage rise. In particular the increment of the wage bill of Departments I and II, equal to $\alpha(W_1 + W_2)$, must unavoidably cause profits of the Department III to rise *pro tanto*. Indeed, the profits of this department consist of the proceeds out of the sale of the wage goods which are not consumed by the workers employed in that department to the workers of Departments I and II. Thus the increment in the wage bill of these deparments, $\alpha(W_1 + W_2)$, means an equal rise in profits of Department III. This may occur either through the rise in output in that department or through the rise of the prices of its products.

As a result the total profits remain unaltered, the loss of the Departments I and II by $\alpha(W_1 + W_2)$ being counterbalanced by an equal gain of the Department III. It follows that no absolute shift from profits to wages occurs and the argument based on Say's law would thus prove fallacious—at least with regard to the short period considered.

The last qualification is essential. For it may be argued that the decline in the volume of investment and capitalists' consumption as a result of the wage rise although not immediate would still come about with delay, say, in the next short period. And this would be true if capitalists at least *decided* to cut their investment and consumption immediately after having agreed to raise wages. But even this is unlikely: for their decisions are based on current experience; and this according to the above will show that no loss in total profits occurs in the short period following the wage rise and thus it will give no reason for a cut in investment and capitalists' consumption in the next period. If a decision for such a cut is not taken right away on the basis of the bare fact of the wage rise, it will not be taken at all. And as a result profits will not shrink in the next period either. The argument on the shift from profits to wages as a result of a wage rise based on Say's law is thus fallacious even if we consider all the ramifications of this event.

The same applies obviously to a wage cut: no increase in profits will occur either in the short period following it or subsequently.

2. So far we assumed that prices of investment goods and consumption goods for capitalists remain unchanged when wages increase, which was in line with the theory of shift from profits to wages to the extent of the wage rise. (The preceding section amounted in a sense to the *reductio ad absurdum* of this theory). In fact, however, this is unlikely to be the case: these prices will rather rise under the impact of the wage increase —perhaps not in the short period following directly the wage rise but subsequently. But to discuss this question as well as other repercussions of the wage rise—or of the wage cut—we want to know more about price formation in the system considered.

We shall first abstract from all semi-monopolistic and monopolistic factors, i.e. we shall assume so called 'perfect competition'. Let me add immediately that this is a most unrealistic assumption not only for the present phase of capitalism but even for the so called competitive capitalist economy of past centuries: surely this competition was always in general very imperfect. Perfect competition when its actual status of a handy model is forgotten becomes a dangerous myth.

As follows from the argument in the preceding section, the

volume of capitalists' investment and consumption is maintained in the short period following the wage rise and consequently thereafter. On the assumption of perfect competition and of supply curves sloping upwards at some point, the rise in wage rates must cause a proportional rise in prices at given levels of respective outputs—perhaps not in the first short period but subsequently. As a result profits in Departments I and II will rise in the same proportion as wages, i.e. $1 + \alpha$ times.

Now it is easy to prove that the volume of production and consumption of wage goods also remains unchanged. Indeed, in such a case profits in Department III as in the other two departments increase in the proportion of the wage rise, i.e. $1 + \alpha$ times; now, as mentioned in section 1, the profits in Department III are equal to the proceeds out of sales of the wage goods to the workers of Departments I and II and therefore they must increase in the same proportion as wages in these departments, i.e. $1 + \alpha$ times. If the volume of production and consumption of wage goods increased or declined, such could not be the case.

Thus with perfect competition the volume of production in all three departments remains unchanged while its value increases in each of them $1 + \alpha$ times. In this proportion thus the total wage bill increases and the total profits, i.e. the distribution of national income remains unaltered.

Consequently, having shown the fallacy of the theory based on Say's law which maintained that wage movements have a direct and full impact upon the distribution of national income, we now arrive at the opposite extreme, that they have no influence whatever upon this distribution. But this conclusion is based on the untenable assumption of perfect competition. In fact only by dropping it and penetrating the world of imperfect competition and oligopolies are we able to arrive at any reasonable conclusion on the impact of bargaining for wages on the distribution of income.†

---

† We abstracted here from the influence of the increase in the price level upon the rate of interest by assuming tacitly that the supply of money by the banks is elastic. Otherwise the higher demand for money would have increased the rate of interest which would affect adversely investment and consequently profits. Such

3. In fact a major part of the economy may be plausibly represented by a model very different from perfect competition. Each firm in an industry arrives at the price of its product p by 'marking up' its direct cost u consisting of average costs of wages *plus* raw materials in order to cover overheads and achieve profits. But this mark-up is dependent on 'competition', i.e. on relation of the ensuing price p to the weighted average price of this product $\bar{p}$ for the industry as a whole. Or:

$$\frac{p-u}{u} = f\left(\frac{\bar{p}}{p}\right) \tag{1}$$

where f is an increasing function: the lower is p in relation to $\bar{p}$, the higher will be fixed the mark up. From formula (1) we obtain:

$$p = u\left[1 + f\left(\frac{\bar{p}}{p}\right)\right] \tag{2}$$

It should be noted that the function f may be different for various firms of an industry. They will reflect semi-monopolistic influences referred to above, resulting from imperfect competition or oligopoly. The more intensive are these factors, the higher $f(\bar{p}/p)$ corresponding to a given relation $\bar{p}/p$. Prices p will be in general different for various firms because of the differences in direct costs u and because of those in the functions f.

The price system is determined. Indeed with s firms in an industry there will be $s+1$ price values to be determined, i.e. $p_1, p_2, \ldots p_s, \bar{p}$, and as many equations: s equations of the type (2) and one determining $\bar{p}$ in terms of $p_1, p_2, \ldots p_s$.

If all direct costs u, with given functions f, increased $1 + \alpha$ times, so do all prices $p_1, p_2, \ldots p_s$. Indeed, this solution satisfies the equations (2) because u by assumption increases $1 + \alpha$ times and $\bar{p}/p$ remains unaltered.

If, however, the direct cost u_k increases only for one firm (again with given functions f), it is easy to see that p_k increases in a lesser proportion because $\bar{p}$ will then not rise in the same proportion as u_k.

effect seems unlikely to be of any greater importance, especially because the changes in the bank rate are reflected on a much reduced scale in the long-term rate of interest.

4. Since prices p for a product are in general not equal, the above applies strictly to imperfect competition or differential oligopoly but not to non-differential oligopoly or monopoly. However, in fact, apart from basic raw materials produced frequently in conditions approaching perfect competition, most of the products *have* differential prices. (Let us not forget that absolutely identical products with the same transport costs but different periods of delivery may have different prices.)

It seems therefore a fairly good approximation to an actual economy if we assume it consisting of the model described above and the sector of basic raw materials conforming in their price formation to that of perfect competition.

Let us now imagine that in a closed system of this type wage rates in all industries increase in the same proportion, $1 + \alpha$ times. It follows easily that all prices will also increase $1 + \alpha$ times *provided that functions f in industries to which they are relevant are unchanged*. It follows that if these conditions were fulfilled we should arrive at the same conclusion as for perfectly competitive economy in section 2—that a general increase in money wages in a closed economy does not change the distribution of national income. The same would apply to the case of the decrease in money wages. However, we shall argue that the functions f do depend on the trade-union activity.

5. High mark-ups in existence will encourage strong trade unions to bargain for higher wages since they know that firms can 'afford' to pay them. If their demands are granted but the functions f are not changed, prices also increase. This would lead to a new round of demands for higher wages and the process would go on with price levels rising. But surely an industry will not like such a process making its products more and more expensive and thus less competitive with products of other industries.† To sum up, trade-union power restrains the mark-ups, i.e. it causes the values $f(\bar{p}/p)$ to be lower than would be the case otherwise.

† Despite the fact that for the sake of simplicity we assumed that all wage rates are raised simultaneously in the same proportion, we consider realistically that bargaining is proceeding by industries.

Now, this power manifests itself in the scale of wage rises demanded and achieved. If an increase in bargaining capacity is demonstrated by spectacular achievements, there is a downward shift in functions $f(\bar{p}/p)$ and the mark-ups' decline. A redistribution of national income from profits to wages will take place then. But this redistribution is much smaller than that which would obtain if prices were stable. The rise in wages is to a great extent 'shifted to consumers'. And 'normal' wage increases will usually leave the functions f unaffected while otherwise mark ups may tend to get higher because of the rise in productivity of labour.

6. Let us imagine that a spectacular wage rise depresses somewhat the mark-ups so that a redistribution of national income from profits to wages occurs. Now from section 1 it follows that profits in Department III will increase in the same proportion as wage rates. But, as there is a redistribution of income from profits to wages as a result of the reduction of mark-ups there, the wage bill in Department III increases more than wage rates, i.e. there is a rise in employment and output there. In consequence output and employment will be unaltered in Departments I and II while they will rise in Department III. Or the volume of investment and capitalists' consumption will not change, but workers' consumption will increase. Such an expansion of total output and employment will be feasible because in fact our model of semi-monopolistic price fixing, as developed in Section 3, presupposes the existence of excess capacities.

As to the (money) value of the wage bill it will clearly increase in a higher proportion than the wage rates. However, total profits will increase *less* than the wage rates: indeed, profits in Department III increase proportionately to the wage rates, employment in Departments I and II being unaltered, but profits in the latter two departments increase less than the wage rates as a result of the decline of mark-ups there.†

† This, however, is subject to the following qualification. As a result of the increase of total output there will be an increase in prices of basic raw materials,

If the trade union power declined the process described above would be reversed. Employment and output in Departments I and II would remain unchanged, but in Department III they would decline. Or the volume of investment and capitalists' consumption would remain unchanged and the consumption of workers would fall. The total output and employment would thus decline. The value of the wage bill would fall more than the wage rates while the value of profits would decline less than the wage rates.†

Since the decline in the mark-ups tends to increase aggregate output, this would cause a rise in prices of basic raw materials, subject to conditions of perfect competition, in relation to wages. As a result the increase in output and employment would be somewhat restrained. In the same fashion this factor would somehow restrain the fall in output and employment caused by the rise of the mark-ups.

It follows from the above that a wage rise showing an increase in the trade union power leads—contrary to the precepts of classical economics—to an increase in employment. And conversely, a fall in wages showing a weakening in their bargaining power leads to a decline in employment. The weakness of trade unions in a depression manifested in permitting wage cuts contributes to deepening of unemployment rather than to relieving it.

7. It follows from the above that the class struggle as reflected in trade-union bargaining may affect the distribution of national income but in a much more sophisticated fashion than expressed by the crude doctrine: when wages are raised, profits fall *pro tanto*. This doctrine proves to be entirely wrong. Such shifts that occur are: (*a*) connected with widespread imperfect competition and oligopoly in capitalist system; and (*b*) they are contained in fairly narrow limits. However, the day-by-day

inter alia those used alike by Department I or II and Department III. This, although not very likely, may offset the influence of the decline in mark-ups in Departments I and II upon the distribution of income between profits and wages. In any case, however, total profits will rise in a lower proportion than total wage bill.

† Subject to a qualification analogous to that stated in the preceding footnote.

bargaining process is an important co-determinant of the distribution of national income.

It should be noted that it is possible to devise other forms of class struggle than wage bargaining, which would affect the distribution of national income in a more direct way. For instance, actions may be undertaken for keeping down the cost of living. The latter might be achieved by price controls which, however, may prove difficult to administer. But there exists an alternative: subsidizing of prices of wage goods which is financed by direct taxation of profits. Such an operation, by the way, will not affect aggregate net profits: the argument is the same as used in section 1 in the case of a wage increase. The same is true of the effect of price controls. And, if such measures cannot be carried out by political parties associated with trade unions in the parliament, the power of the trade unions may be used to mobilize supporting strike movements. The classical day-by-day bargaining for wages is not the only way of influencing the distribution of national income to the advantage of the workers.

8. The redistribution of income from profits to wages, as described in the last two sections, is feasible only if excess capacity is in existence. Otherwise it is impossible to increase wages in relation to prices of wage goods because prices are determined by demand, and functions f become defunct. We return then to the position described in section 2 where the wage rise could not affect a redistribution of income.

Price control of wage goods will lead under the circumstances to scarcities of goods and haphazard distribution. Also subsidizing prices of wage goods (financed by direct taxation of profits) can reduce prices only in the longer run by stimulating investment in wage good industries.

It should be noted, however, that even contemporary capitalism, where deep depressions are avoided as a result of Government intervention, is in general still fairly remote from such a state of full utilisation of resources. This is best shown by the fact that prices of finished goods *are* fixed on a cost basis rather than determined by demand.

15. TREND AND THE
BUSINESS CYCLE

[1968]

I. INTRODUCTION

The contemporary theory of growth of capitalist economies tends to consider this problem in terms of a moving equilibrium rather than adopting an approach similar to that applied in the theory of business cycles. The latter consists of establishing two relations: one based on the impact of the effective demand generated by investment upon profits and the national income; and the other showing the determination of investment decisions by, broadly speaking, the level and the rate of change of economic activity. The first relation does not involve now particularly intricate questions. The second, to my mind, remains the central *pièce de résistance* of economics.

I do not see why this approach should be abolished in the face of the problem of long-run growth. In fact, the long-run trend is but a slowly changing component of a chain of short-period situations; it has no independent entity, and the two basic relations mentioned above should be formulated in such a way as to yield the trend cum business-cycle phenomenon. It is true that the task is incomparably more difficult than in the case of another abstraction, that of the 'pure business cycle' and, as will be seen below, the results of such an inquiry are less 'mechanistic'. This, however, is no excuse for dropping this approach, which seems to me the only key to the realistic analysis of the dynamics of a capitalist economy.

I myself approached this problem in my *Theory of Economic Dynamics*† and my 'Observations on the Theory of Growth'‡ in

† George Allen and Unwin, London, 1954.   ‡ *Economic Journal*, March 1962.

a manner which now I do not consider entirely satisfactory: I started from developing a theory of the 'pure business cycle' in a stationary economy, and at a later stage I modified the respective equations to get the trend into the picture. By this separation of short-period and long-run influences I missed certain repercussions of technical progress which affect the dynamic process as a whole. I shall now try to avoid splitting my argument into these two stages just as much as applying the approach of moving equilibrium to the problem of growth.

2. ASSUMPTIONS

Our simplifying assumptions fall into a few categories. We assume a closed system and abstract from government activities, concentrating deliberately on a self-contained *laisser faire* capitalist economy. We abstract as well from workers' savings, which are definitely unimportant.

We also make some assumptions for the mere sake of simplicity which *are* unrealistic; however, if the respective factors were taken into account this, while complicating the argument, would not change it basically. We abstract from the time-lag in consumer expenditure. This again is realistic with regard to workers' consumption but not so with regard to that of capitalists. However, as long as the time-lag between investment decisions and investment is emphasised, disregarding that between profits and capitalists' consumption does not distort the analysis.

Similarly, we abstract from overhead labour (consisting mainly of salary earners) and thus assume that all labour receipts are prime costs. This would again distort the changes in the relation between investment and the national income in the course of the trade cycle were it not for the fact that we distinguish in the capitalists' consumption a part which does not depend on the current level of profits. This element leads to proportionate changes in gross investment in the course of the business cycle being higher than those in profits and the national income. Thus the factor of overhead labour, having similar repercussions, may be disregarded without distorting the familiar pattern of the trade cycle.

Finally, the most drastic simplification is abstracting from changes in inventories so that investment is exclusively in fixed capital. Again such an assumption would not be acceptable if not for the fact that—as will be seen below—our formula for investment decisions includes a member proportionate to the increment of profits in the year considered. Since the increase in inventories may be assumed to be proportionate to that of the national income which bears in our model a stable relation to profits, this prevents also in this case a distortion of the dynamics of the system.

In short: we do make drastic simplifications to concentrate the attention of the reader on the most essential issues without, however, throwing out the baby along with the bath-water.

3. INVESTMENT, SAVING, PROFITS AND NATIONAL INCOME

Let us denote gross investment in fixed capital in a given year by I, gross saving by S, capitalists' consumption by C_K and gross profits by P (all these magnitudes are meant in constant prices). Since the system is closed, the government expenditure and revenue is disregarded, the workers are assumed not to save and increases in inventories are abstracted from, we have

$$S = I \qquad (15.1)$$

and
$$P = I' + C_K \qquad (15.2)$$

Moreover, we may plausibly postulate, neglecting the time-lag between capitalists' consumption and profits, that

$$C_K = \lambda P + A \qquad (15.3)$$

where λ is a rather small fraction and where A is a certain slowly changing magnitude dependent on past economic and social developments. It may be called a semi-autonomous variable because we shall not try to relate it to any other variables entering our argument, in which therefore it will be considered, at least at the present stage, a slowly changing function of time $A(t)$. From the equations (15.2) and (15.3) it follows directly

$$P_t = \frac{I_t + A(t)}{1 - \lambda} \tag{15.4}$$

or denoting $1/(1 - \lambda)$ by m

$$P_t = m(I_t + A(t)) \tag{15.4'}$$

where m is greater but not much greater than 1.

Next we shall deal briefly with the relation between profits P and the gross national income Y. We shall consider the ratio P/Y which we denote by q, a parameter which, although in the long run it may be subject to important changes, will be treated in our equations as a constant. The justification of this is as follows:

First, since we abstract from the overhead labour, all labour costs are prime costs. But, as I indicated time and again in my previous work, the relative share of labour prime costs in the national income depends on the mark-ups over the prime costs and the relation between unit wage costs and prices of basic raw-materials.†

Next, as long as the resources of the economy are far from being fully utilised—and this I believe to be the typical condition of a developed capitalist economy—the mark-ups are determined by semi-monopolistic and monopolistic factors which I nicknamed 'degree of monopoly'. It is this term, I think, that facilitated the dismissal of the theory as being 'tautological'. However, in the *Theory of Economic Dynamics* I showed, I believe, that in any case no problem of *tautology* is involved.‡ If the price is not determined by the equilibrium of supply at full utilisation of equipment, on the one hand, and demand, on the other—the prices are *fixed* by the firms on the basis of the average prime costs and the average price of the product group in question.§

† Cf., e.g. Chapter 6, pp. 62–4.   ‡ Cf. Chapter 5, pp. 43–52.
§ Cf. Chapter 5, pp. 44–9.

By assuming $q = (P/Y)$ constant we confine our discussion to the case when the pricing process, and changes in the ratio of unit wage costs to prices of basic raw materials, do not cause a change in q. Of course, the assumption that q is a parameter which under conditions described *may* be constant is incompatible with the approach considering q to be just the instrument of securing—through price flexibility in relation to demand—the full utilisation of resources. (Business cycles appear in such an approach as merely 'lapses from full employment' resulting from the imperfection of this instrument.) However, we consider such an approach utterly unrealistic, since a *laisser faire* capitalist economy used to achieve a more or less full utilisation of resources only at the top of a boom, and frequently not even then. Nor did these full-employment booms fill a major part of the cycle.

Thus we shall stick to our assumption and postulate

$$Y = \frac{P}{q} \qquad (15.5)$$

4. INVESTMENT DECISIONS (*a*)

We shall make an attempt here to attack the problem of determination of investment decisions in a somewhat novel way. But to prepare the ground for it we have to introduce first a concept of that level of investment in a given year at which the new equipment would yield a certain definite gross rate of profit. This 'standard rate of profit' is the reciprocal of the so-called 'pay off period' during which the capital invested is recovered. Let us denote this rate by π. Let us, moreover, denote that level of new investment which would 'fetch' under conditions prevailing in the year considered the rate of profit by π by $I(\pi)$. It is clear that the higher, *ceteris paribus*, the level of investment, the lower is the rate of profit it 'fetches'. Thus if the rate of profit actually yielded by new equipment is higher than π, then $I(\pi)$ is higher than actual investment I, and vice versa; and obviously $I(\pi) = I$ if these rates are equal.

We shall now try to establish the determinants of $I(\pi)$. If we abstract for a moment from the increase in productivity due to technical progress, $I(\pi)$ may be assumed to be proportionate to the increment in 'real' profits from the beginning to the end of the year considered, which we denote by ΔP. Since ample unused productive capacities are postulated to be in existence, new investment will capture only a part of profits $n\Delta P$, where n is a rather small fraction. Thus since $I(n)$ is defined as that level of investment which 'fetches' the rate of profit π, we shall have in the case presently discussed $I(\pi) = n\Delta P/\pi$.

Let us introduce the influence of technical progress now. With 'real' gross profits in the year considered P and the 'real' gross national income Y we obtain for 'real' labour costs $Y-P$. This will be also approximately the level of the labour costs associated with old equipment because the new capacities put to use in the year considered are small in relation to those of the total existing capital equipment. Now during the year considered the 'real' labour costs associated with old equipment will rise as a result of the increase in productivity caused by technical progress, Y and P being expressed in constant prices.

In consequence of this rise profits yielded by old equipment will fall. If the price of a product were uniform the transfer of output would occur merely through some obsolete equipment going out of use and the transfer of profits through the reduction of the profit margins for the produce of working old equipment. In fact, however, the market prices of the products are not uniform and the transfer of profits occurs also in part through the transfer of output of working old equipment to the new one. It follows that profits yielded by old equipment will fall in the year considered by $\alpha(Y-P)$, where α is the higher the greater the rate of increase in productivity resulting from technical progress.

Now the loss in profits yielded by old equipment is—given the total profits P—the gain in profits captured by the new plant. In fact, therefore the profits captured by the level of investment $I(\pi)$ will be $n\Delta P + \alpha(Y-P)$ rather than $n\Delta P$, and the corresponding modified formula for $I(\pi)$ is

$$I(\pi) = \frac{n\Delta P + \alpha(Y-P)}{\pi} \qquad (15.6)$$

As a first approximation to the problem of the level of investment 'fetching' a 'standard rate of profit' π we shall treat n and α as constants. The equation conveys then in any case the fact that the level of investment 'capturing' the rate of profit π depends on two basic determinants: the increment in total profits and the transfer of profits from old to new equipment, resulting from technical progress.

According to the equation (15.5)

$$\alpha(Y-P) = \alpha\left(\frac{P}{q}-P\right) = P\alpha\left(\frac{1}{q}-1\right) = \delta P \qquad (15.7)$$

where we denote $\alpha[(1/q)-1]$ by δ.† Thus we may write the formula (15.6) in the form

$$I(\pi) = \frac{n\Delta P + \delta P}{\pi} \qquad (15.8)$$

5. INVESTMENT DECISIONS (b)

We shall approach the problem of investment decisions in two stages. In this section we shall abstract from a certain rather complicated factor which, however, is of considerable importance. We shall introduce it in the next section.

We assume that the investment decisions in a given year depend on two sorts of considerations: (a) those concerning the gross entrepreneurial savings (including those out of dividends of the controlling groups of shareholders of joint-stock companies) accruing in this period, and (b) those concerning the prerequisites for their reinvestment.

---

† As profits yielded by equipment decline by a fraction δ per annum as a result of obsolescence, it is in fact the rate of depreciation in the literal sense, because by so much decreases the profit-yielding capacity of capital equipment, and the same may be said about its 'real value' (cf. section 10).

The former are tied with the problem of the entrepreneurial capital being the basis of investment because of limited capital markets and the 'increasing risk' involved in making use of it (which was discussed in Chapter 9).

The considerations concerning the prerequisites for reinvestment of entrepreneurial savings—i.e. whether the investment decisions taken in a given year are to be equal to entrepreneurial savings, exceed them or fall short of them—are closely related to the idea of the 'normal rate of profit' π on new investment. We assume that if such investment that would capture in the year considered the rate of profit π is equal to what was the actual investment in this period, i.e. $I(\pi) = I$, the entrepreneurial savings are just being reinvested. If $I(\pi) > I$ more than that is invested, and vice versa. Thus denoting investment decisions taken in the period considered by D and entrepreneurial savings by E, we may write

$$D = E + r(I(\pi) - I)$$

where r is a coefficient measuring the intensity of the reaction of the entrepreneurs to the difference $I(\pi) - I$.

Substituting in this equation the expression for $I(\pi)$ as given by formula (15.8), we obtain

$$D = E + r\left(\frac{n\Delta P + \delta P}{\pi} - I\right)$$

We shall assume that the gross entrepreneurial savings bear a constant relation to the rentier savings (which are much smaller). We thus have

$$E = eS \qquad (15.9)$$

where e is less but not much less than one and taking into consideration $S = I$ (equation 15.1) we obtain

$$D = eI + r\left(\frac{n\Delta P + \delta P}{\pi} - I\right)$$

The characteristic feature of this formula for investment decisions D per unit of time as compared with other approaches to this problem (including my previous work on the subject) is the

member δP which accounts explicitly for the stimulus to investment due to higher productivity of labour in the new plant
enabling them to capture profits from old equipment. A very
imperfect substitute for allowing for this factor in other theories
(including my own) was to carry the argument in terms of net
rather than gross investment.

6. INVESTMENT DECISIONS (c)

The formula for investment decisions must be still supplemented
in order to account for an additional factor. The above argument is based on the idea that entrepreneurs scrutinise how the
new investment 'is doing' in terms of profitability, and on this
basis form a decision whether just to reinvest their savings, to
exceed their level or to fall short of it: this depends on whether
the rate of profit on new actual investment proves to be equal,
higher or lower than the 'standard rate' π. An important
element of how the new investment 'is doing' is the rise in
productivity due to technical progress, which causes a transfer
of profits from old to new equipment. But there is still another
effect of innovations.

In the year considered new inventions come within the com-
pass of the entrepreneurs. Thus they expect to do better out of
their investment than those whose investment materialised in
the year considered. In fact, this will not prove true for the
investing entrepreneurs as a body: if the increase in productivity
is not accelerated the investment materialising in the next year
will not be more profitable on the average than that in the
present one. Nevertheless, those entrepreneurs who are first to
avail themselves of the technical novelties *will* do better than
the average.

To account for this additional stimulus to investment which
is a direct outcome of innovations we shall add to the right-hand
side of the formula for investment decisions a slowly changing
magnitude depending—similarly to the stable part of capitalists' consumption—on past economic, social and technological

developments. This semi-autonomous variable may be considered, at least at the present stage, a slowly changing function of time $B(t)$. We thus have

$$D_t = eI_t + r\left(\frac{n\Delta P_t + \delta P_t}{\pi} - I_t\right) + B(t) \qquad (15.10)$$

7. THE EQUATION OF DYNAMICS OF INVESTMENT

Denoting the time-lag between investment decisions and actual investment by τ, we have

$$D_t = I_{t+\tau} \qquad (15.11)$$

and thus we may write equation (15.10) as

$$I_{t+\tau} = (e-r)I_t + \frac{r}{\pi}(n\Delta P_t + \delta P_t) + B(t)$$

We shall now substitute into this equation profits expressed in terms of investment in accordance with the formula (4′), i.e. $P_t = m(I_t + A(t))$. We obtain

$$I_{t+\tau} = \left(e - r + \frac{r}{\pi}m\delta\right)I_t + \frac{r}{\pi}mn\Delta I_t$$

$$+ \frac{r}{\pi}m\delta A(t) + \frac{r}{\pi}mn\Delta A(t) + B(t) \qquad (15.12)$$

Let us now introduce the notations

$$a = e - r + \frac{r}{\pi}m\delta = e - r\left(1 - m\frac{\delta}{\pi}\right) \qquad (15.13)$$

$$b = \frac{r}{\pi}mn \qquad (15.14)$$

$$F(t) = \frac{r}{\pi}m\delta\Delta(t) + \frac{r}{\pi}mn\Delta A(t) + B(t)$$

$$= \frac{r}{\pi}m\delta A(t)\left(1 + \frac{n}{\delta}\frac{\Delta A(t)}{A(t)}\right) + B(t) \qquad (15.15)$$

We shall assume $a < 1$, which is plausible in view of the likely values for the parameters involved. First, e being the relative share of entrepreneurial savings in total savings is less than one. Moreover, $m(\delta/\pi)$ is very likely to be less than one as well. Indeed, m is not much more than one (see section 3). But π is very probably much higher than δ for the following reasons. The 'standard rate of profit' is the reciprocal of the so-called 'pay off period' during which the entrepreneurs expect 'normally' to recover the capital invested. For the economy as a whole it may be assumed to be not more than, say, six to seven years, thus π may be assumed to be about 15%. Now, according to equation (15.7), $\delta = \alpha[(1/q) - 1]$, where α is of the order of the annual increase in the 'real' labour costs associated with old equipment and q the relative share of profits in the national income. It is clear that δ can hardly exceed 5%. We thus arrive at the conclusion that $e < 1$ and $r(1 - m[\delta/\pi]) > 0$, from which follows directly $a < 1$.

As to the function $F(t)$ determined by equation (15.15), it may be assumed to be a slowly changing function of time determined by past economic, social and technological developments. Indeed, $A(t)$ and $B(t)$ were assumed to be this type of functions. Moreover, we interpret the slowly changing function of time as one whose annual increment is a small fraction of its level. We postulate

$$\left| \frac{n}{\delta} \frac{\Delta A(t)}{A(t)} \right|$$

to be small in relation to one (n is a rather small fraction; cf. section 4). It will be easily seen that then $F(t)$ is a slowly changing function in this sense as well.

We may now write our equation of dynamics of investment in the form

$$I_{t+\tau} = aI_t + b\Delta I_t + F(t) \qquad (15.12')$$

where a, b and $F(t)$ are determined by equations (15.13), (15.14) and (15.15); a is assumed to be less than one and $F(t)$—a slowly changing function of time rooted in past developments.

8. TREND AND BUSINESS-CYCLE
COMPONENTS OF INVESTMENT

On certain assumptions about the slowly changing function $F(t)$ equation (15.12′) has as a particular solution a positive steady function of time y_t. If we subtract from equation (15.12′) the equation

$$y_{t+\tau} = ay_t + b\Delta y_t + F(t) \qquad (15.16)$$

we obtain $\quad I_{t+\tau} - y_{t+\tau} = a\,(I_t - y_t) + b\Delta(I_t - y_t) \quad (15.17)$

The latter equation, however, is known to generate cyclical fluctuations of $I_t - y_t$. (The necessary condition for this is $a < 1$; this is fulfilled according to the argument in section 7).†

The problem of determining y_t is rather intricate. We shall assume $F(t)$ to be such a type of function that equation (15.16) is satisfied by a y_t steadily but slowly changing (which means that $|\,(\Delta y_t / y_t)\,| \leqslant \beta$ where β is a small fraction). Such functions $F\,(t)$ do exist because the condition is fulfilled for an exponential function $F(t) = ce^{\beta t}$. Indeed, equation (15.16) is satisfied then by

$$y_t = \frac{ce^{\beta t}}{1 - a + e^{\beta \tau} - 1 - b\beta}$$

where the denominator is positive for a sufficiently small β. The functions of the type mentioned constitute, however, a broader class covering what is, roughly speaking, the nearly exponential functions, i.e. functions differing very little from exponential functions in short periods although this may not be the case in sufficiently long stretches of time.

Let us write equation (15.16) in the form

$$y_{t+\tau} - ay_t - b\Delta y_t = y_{t+\tau} - y_t + (1 - a)y_t - b\Delta y_t = F(t)$$

from which follows directly

$$y_t = \frac{F(t)}{1 - a + \dfrac{y_{t+\tau} - y_t - b\Delta y_t}{y_t}}$$

† See, for instance, Chapter 10.

Since y_t is according to our assumptions a positive slowly changing function of time and the time-lag between investment and investment decisions τ is only a few years we may write

$$\left| \frac{y_{t+\tau} - y_t - b\Delta y_t}{y_t} \right| \leqslant \gamma$$

where γ is also rather small. We thus obtain for the particular solution of equation $(15.12')$

$$y_t = \frac{d_t}{1-a} F(t) \qquad (15.18)$$

where
$$\frac{1}{1 + \dfrac{\gamma}{1-a}} \leqslant d_t \leqslant \frac{1}{1 - \dfrac{\gamma}{1-a}} \qquad (15.19)$$

Let us denote the maximum of $|\Delta F(t)/F(t)|$ by ζ. It follows from the condition (15.19) that the average rate of change of y_t over a period of several years cannot differ much from that of $F(t)$, and thus cannot exceed much in absolute value the maximum rate of change ζ of $F(t)$.

Or to put it a little differently for a particular case: if $F(t)$ shows an increasing tendency over a several years' period the average rate of growth of y_t over this period is approximately equal to that of $F(t)$, and thus cannot exceed ζ much.

We may write now
$$I_t = y_t + (I_t - y_t) \qquad (15.20)$$

where y_t is the trend component (which is not necessarily increasing) while $I_t - y_t$ is the cyclical component corresponding to the equation (15.17).

From the formula $(15.4')$ we may derive a corresponding equation for profits.

$$P_t = m(I_t + A(t)) = m(y_t + A(t)) + m(I_t - y_t) \qquad (15.21)$$

Obviously $m(y_t + A(t))$ is the trend component and $m(I_t - y_t)$ the business-cycle component of profits.

For the national income we obtain from formula (15.5)

$$Y_t = \frac{P_t}{q} = \frac{m}{q}(y_c + A(t)) + \frac{m}{q}(I_t - y_t) \qquad (15.22)$$

9. DISCUSSION OF THE TREND COMPONENT

For the time being we know of the trend components of investment, profits and the national income merely that they are positive functions of time which in longer periods exhibit approximately the same average rate of change as $F(t)$. We cannot say in the light of the above argument whether they increase or decline. The latter case is, by the way, by no means absurd: it may in fact happen. We shall now try to outline an economic situation in which there does exist a tendency for an increasing trend.

Imagine that for a certain fairly long initial period of s years profit, and thus also national income, showed a significant increase after elimination of the cyclical fluctuations. It is a plausible assumption that after this period both the stable part of capitalists' consumption $A(t)$ and the immediate impact of innovations upon investment $B(t)$ will tend to grow for a number of years unless there were some changes in social patterns or in the stream of inventions to upset this tendency. This, however, means that $F(t)$ will also show an increase in this period and that according to section 8 the trend component of investment y_t, as well as that of profits and the national income, will grow. Thus profits and the national income will exhibit a rising tendency in a s-year period later than the initial one which will make for a continuation of the rise in $A(t)$ and $B(t)$. In this way the tendency of the economy for growth proves to be self-sustaining.

As said above, the average rate of growth of y_t over a longer period cannot much exceed ζ, the maximum rate of change of $F(t)$. If the maximum rate of change of the stable part of capitalists' consumption $A(t)$ does not exceed ζ either, the same is true—according to equations (15.21) and (15.22)—of profits and the national income.

So far we have dealt with the problem of the trend of gross investment, profits and the national income. Is it possible, adopting our approach, to say anything on such subjects as the rate of growth of the stock of fixed capital and the 'trend value' of the degree of utilisation of capacity? We shall argue that for these problems the degree of monopoly (influencing considerably the relative share of profits in the national income) and the ceiling ζ of the rate of change of the function $F(t)$ are of crucial importance. Before, however, embarking upon this discussion it is necessary to give a definition of net investment and the stock of fixed capital.

10. DEPRECIATION, THE STOCK OF FIXED CAPITAL AND NET INVESTMENT

We shall define the rate of depreciation for a capitalist economy in the literal sense of the word. According to section 4, profits yielded by the old equipment diminish by a fraction δ per annum as a result of technical progress. Thus the profit-yielding capacity of equipment declines by the same fraction. The 'real value' of old equipment may thus be plausibly assumed to decline each year in the proportion $1 - \delta$.† Thus the 'trend real value' of the stock of fixed capital K_t may be evaluated as follows

$$K_t = y_t + y_{t-1}(1 - \delta) + y_{t-2}(1 - \delta)^2 + \qquad (15.23)$$

and the depreciation in the year t as δK_t. Thus for the 'trend value' of net investment we have

$$\Delta K_t = y_t - \delta K_t \qquad (15.24)$$

and for the respective rate of growth of the stock of fixed capital

$$\frac{\Delta K_t}{K_t} = \frac{y_t}{K_t} - \delta \qquad (15.24')$$

The approach to the problem of depreciation outlined here is, I think, more realistic than that based on equipment actually scrapped. Equipment may not be scrapped, but, being obsolete, may be of very little practical use, which shows the weakness of the definition in question. What we suggest here is rather close to the business concept, although, of course, δ need not be

† Cf. footnote section 4.

12-2

assumed equivalent to the conventional rates of depreciation used mainly for the sake of calculating the taxable income.†

Equation (15.22) permits us to estimate on the basis of our assumptions about the function $F(t)$ the lower limit of the stock of capital K_t. Taking into account the formula (15.18), we may write this equation in the form

$$K_t = \frac{1}{1-a}\left(d_t F(t) + d_{t-1} F(t-1)(1-\delta)\right)$$
$$+ d_{t-2} F(t-2)(1-\delta)^2 \ldots).$$

Since according to (15.19)

$$d_t \geqslant \frac{1}{1+\dfrac{\gamma}{1-a}}$$

and $F(t)$ cannot increase at a rate higher than ζ, we have the inequality

$$K_t \geqslant \frac{F(t)}{(1-a)\left(1+\dfrac{\gamma}{1-a}\right)}\left(1+\frac{1-\delta}{1+\zeta}+\left(\frac{1-\delta}{1+\zeta}\right)^2 \ldots\right)$$

$$= \frac{F(t)}{(1-a+\gamma)}\frac{1}{1-\dfrac{1-\delta}{1+\zeta}}$$

$$= \frac{(1+\zeta)F(t)}{(1-a+\gamma)(\zeta+\delta)} > \frac{F(t)}{(1-a+\gamma)(\zeta+\delta)}$$

But from equations (15.18) and (15.19) it follows that

$$y_t \leqslant \frac{F(t)}{(1-a)\left(1-\dfrac{\gamma}{1-a}\right)} = \frac{F(t)}{1-a-\gamma}$$

Thus
$$\frac{y_t}{K_t} < (\zeta+\delta)\frac{1-a-\gamma}{1-a+y} \tag{15.25}$$

† It is easy to see from equation (15.16) that in the case when $F(t)$ is a constant F, the value of y_t will be as well a constant equal to $F/(1-a)$. According to equation (15.23) the fixed capital K_t will be in such a case $F/(1-a)\delta$ and thus the depreciation δK_t is equal to $F/(1-a)$ or to gross investment. Consequently this will be the case of a stationary economy in which cyclical fluctuations will take place around the depreciation level.

and
$$\frac{\Delta K_t}{K_t} = \frac{y_t}{K_t} - \delta < \zeta \frac{1-a+y}{1-a-y} + \delta \frac{2\gamma}{1-a-y} \qquad (15.26)$$

It follows that ζ the maximum rate of change of $F(t)$ is a very important factor in the determination of the ceiling of the rate of capital accumulation. Since γ is rather small in relation $1-a$, it will be easily seen that this ceiling is close to ζ.

10. THE LONG-RUN UTILISATION OF PRODUCTIVE CAPACITY

It follows from the argument of the preceding section that it is difficult to give a precise definition of productive capacity. There are elements of existing capital equipment that could produce only at very high costs and are of little practical importance. Leaving aside for a moment the possible variability of the technique of production, we may plausibly assume a rough proportionality between 'practical productive capacity' and the stock of fixed capital K as defined above. Indeed, the obsolete elements are reduced in importance by continuous depreciation of their volume by a fraction δ per annum. Thus the productive capacity would be represented by hK where the coefficient h reflects the average technique of production.

Adopting this definition of productive capacity, we may now discuss the problem of the 'trend degree of utilisation of equipment'. The trend component of the national income is, according to equation (15.22),

$$\frac{m}{q} [y_t + A(t)] \quad \text{or} \quad \frac{m}{q} y_t \left(1 + \frac{A(t)}{y_t}\right)$$

Thus the degree of utilisation of productive capacity u_t may be represented as

$$u_t = \frac{\dfrac{m}{q} y_t \left(1 + \dfrac{A(t)}{y_t}\right)}{hK_t} = \frac{m}{hq} \frac{y_t}{K_t} \left(1 + \frac{A(t)}{y_t}\right) \qquad (15.27)$$

Taking into consideration the formula (15.25), setting the ceiling for y_t/K_t, we obtain

$$u_t < \frac{m}{h}\left(1 + \frac{A_t}{y_t}\right)\frac{1-a+\gamma}{1-a-\gamma}\frac{\zeta+\delta}{q} \qquad (15.28)$$

Thus the ceiling of the degree of utilisation of equipment will to a great extent depend on the ratio $(\delta+\zeta)/q$, which we shall examine below in more detail.

It is to be recalled that according to equation (15.7)

$$\delta = \alpha\left(\frac{1}{q}-1\right)$$

i.e. the higher the relative share of profits in the national income, the lower the impact of the increase in 'real costs' associated with old equipment on the rate of decline of the respective profits δ. If follows directly

$$\frac{\zeta+\delta}{q} = \frac{1}{q}\left[\zeta+a\left(\frac{1}{q}-1\right)\right]$$

Thus the utilisation of equipment is considerably affected by the level of q (depending to a great extent on the 'degree of monopoly') and ζ the maximum rate of growth of $F(t)$.† This can be easily illustrated by the following examples:

ζ	0·05	0·05	0·04
α	0·04	0·04	0·04
δ	0·45	0·50	0·50
$\dfrac{\zeta+\delta}{q}$	0·22	0·18	0·16

It is clear that certain combinations of q and ζ will result in a chronic under-utilisation of equipment which was a frequent phenomenon in developed capitalist economies.

† The level of q and ζ need not affect significantly $A(t)/y_t$ and $(1-a+\gamma/1-a-\gamma)$, which also enter the expression for the ceiling of the degree of utilisation determined by formula (15.28).

II. CONCLUDING REMARKS

It follows from the above that in our approach the rate of growth at a given time is a phenomenon rooted in past economic, social and technological developments rather than determined fully by the coefficients of our equations as is the case with the business cycle. This is, indeed, very different from the approach of purely 'mechanistic' theories (based frequently on such fallacious *a priori* assumptions as a constant degree of long-run utilisation of equipment), but seems to me much closer to the realities of the process of development. To my mind future inquiry into the problems of growth should be directed not towards doing without such semi-autonomous magnitudes as $A(t)$ and $B(t)$ but rather towards treating also the coefficients used in our equations (m, n, δ, q) as slowly changing variables rooted in past development of the system.

STATISTICAL APPENDIX

A. NOTES TO CHAPTERS 5 AND 6

Note 1. Data for the period 1899–1914 are given below for: (*a*) the value of fixed capital in U.S. manufacturing according to Paul H. Douglas, *The Theory of Wages*; (*b*) U.S. manufacturing production according to the National Bureau of Economic Research; and (*c*) the value added minus wages in U.S. manufacturing according to the Census of Manufactures.

Year	Value of fixed capital			Production	Value added minus wages in current values
	Book value	At reproduction cost	At constant prices		
1899	100	100	100	100	100
1904	137	136	138	124	130
1909	203	216	198	158	180
1914	256	280	240	186	205

Note 2. The ratio of proceeds to prime costs, the ratio of the materials bill to the wage bill and the relative share of wages in the value added in U.S. manufacturing discussed in Chapters 5 and 6 are based on the U.S. Census of Manufactures. The Census underwent considerable changes both in scope and method. In order to assure reasonable comparability over the period considered (1899–1937) the series were 'linked' in the years in which changes occurred. 1899 was chosen as the base year. Changes in the scope of the Census took place in that year and in 1914. Since for these two years data were available both on the 'old' and the 'new' basis, it was possible to 'link' all the years to the base year 1899. There were also several changes in the method of the Census: (*a*) In 1929, 1931 and 1933 the so-called work and shop supplies were included in the value added

rather than in the cost of materials as was the case in other years. This item, according to the Census of 1904, where it is shown separately, amounted to about 0·9 per cent of the cost of materials. In order to allow approximately for this change, costs of materials in 1929, 1931 and 1933 were accordingly reduced and the value added was increased. (*b*) Prior to 1931 the tax on tobacco manufactures was included in the value added while from 1931 onwards this item was incorporated in the cost of materials. Since for 1931 both variants were given, it was possible to 'link' 1931 and the subsequent years to the base year 1899. (*c*) Prior to 1935 the cost of work given out was included in the value added, while from 1935 onwards this item was included in the cost of materials. Since for 1935 both variants were given, it was possible to link 1935 and the subsequent years to the base year 1899. The figures obtained as a result of the above adjustments are given for selected years in the following table.

Year	Ratio of proceeds to prime costs (%)	Ratio of materials bill to wage bill (%)	Relative share of wages in value added (%)
1879	122·5	382	47·8
1889	131·7	291	44·6
1899	133·3	337	40·7
1914	131·6	370	40·2
1923	133·0	329	41·3
1929	139·4	346	36·2
1931	143·3	314	35·7
1933	142·8	331	35·0
1935	136·6	349	37·9
1937	136·3	338	38·6

Note 3. The series of the ratio of proceeds to prime costs in U.S. manufacturing, assuming stable industrial composition, was calculated by using a chain system. For instance, the ratio of proceeds to prime costs in 1889 was calculated on the assumption that the relative shares of major industrial groups in the aggregate proceeds as of 1879 obtained; this figure divided by

the actual ratio of proceeds to prime costs in 1879 gave the 'link' 1889/1879. Then the 'link' 1899/1889 was similarly derived on the assumption that the relative industrial shares as of 1889 obtained and so on. The year 1899 was chosen as base in the sense that for that year the 'adjusted' ratio of proceeds to prime costs is identical with the actual ratio. The 'adjusted' series could then be built up by means of the 'links'.

The series of the ratio of the materials bill to the wage bill, assuming stable industrial composition of the materials bill, was similarly obtained. 1899 was again chosen as the base year in the above sense.

The 'adjusted' series of the relative share of wages in the value added, w', was calculated from the 'adjusted' ratio of proceeds to prime costs, k', and the 'adjusted' ratio of the materials bill to the wage bill, j', by means of the formula:

$$w' = \frac{1}{1 + (k' - 1)(j' + 1)} \qquad (6.1')$$

(see p. 63). As k' is calculated on the assumption of stable industrial composition of the *proceeds* and j' on the assumption of stable industrial composition of the *materials bill*, w' is the relative share of wages on the assumption of stable industrial composition of the *value added* (the latter being the difference between proceeds and the materials bill). The series k', j' and w' are given in Tables 6.1 and 6.3.

Note 4. The following indices for the United States during the period 1929–41 are given below: (*a*) The index of the wage bill in manufacturing according to U.S. Department of Commerce *Survey of Current Business*, which agrees with the Census of Manufactures for the Census years. (*b*) The index of the wage and salary bill in agriculture, mining, construction, transport, and services according to U.S. Department of Commerce *National Income Supplement to Survey of Current Business*, 1951. (*c*) The combined index of these two series is taken to approximate the index of aggregate wages (see p. 72). The weights adopted are 1 : 1; the wage and salary bills of manufacturing, on the one hand, and of the industries enumerated under (*b*) on the other hand, were approximately equal in 1929, and it may be assumed that the respective wage bills also did not differ very much. (*d*) The index of the gross income of the private sector according to the *National Income Supplement*.

Year	Wage bill in manufacturing	Wage and salary bill in agriculture, mining, construction, transport and services	Combined index	Gross income of the private sector
1929	100	100	100	100
1930	80·9	90·6	85·7	86·0
1931	61·4	74·0	67·7	67·6
1932	42·3	55·0	48·6	48·3
1933	45·4	49·5	47·4	45·3
1934	58·4	55·6	57·0	54·1
1935	67·1	60·5	63·8	62·9
1936	77·7	69·6	73·6	70·1
1937	92·8	77·1	84·9	79·7

Note 5. Wages plus salaries and the gross income of the private sector in the United States in the period 1929–41 according to the *National Income Supplement* are given on p. 188. (It is on these data that the first column in Table 6.7 is based.) It should be noticed that in the national balance sheet given in the *Supplement* there is a statistical discrepancy between national product derived from the income side and from the expenditure side. The figure of gross income in the second column is derived from income statistics. In order to obtain consistent data this figure is adjusted for the statistical discrepancy. (In this way we charge the statistical error fully to the income side which is justified by the fact that the data on expenditures are on the whole more reliable than those on incomes.) The adjusted gross income of the private sector is given in the third column. The adjusted wages plus salaries are assumed to be proportionate to the adjusted gross income and thus the relative share of the former in the latter is not altered by the adjustment.

Year	Private wages and salaries	Gross income of the private sector	Adjusted gross income of the private sector	Adjusted private wages and salaries
		(Billions of current dollars)		
1929	45·2	90·4	90·4	45·2
1930	40·7	77·8	77·1	40·4
1931	33·6	61·1	62·3	34·2
1932	25·3	43·7	45·1	26·1
1933	23·7	40·9	42·2	24·4
1934	27·4	49·0	49·8	27·9
1934	30·0	56·9	56·5	29·8
1936	33·9	68·4	64·2	34·3
1937	38·4	72·1	71·1	37·9
1938	34·6	65·0	64·9	34·5
1939	37·5	70·1	68·8	36·8
1940	41·1	79·0	77·4	40·3
1941	51·5	100·2	98·6	50·7

Note 6. The adjusted gross income of the private sector is deflated below by the index implicit in the deflation of the gross product of the private sector. (This index was obtained by dividing the current value of the gross product of the private sector by its value in constant prices as given in the *Supplement.*)

Year	Price index implicit in deflation of gross product of the private sector 1939 = 100	Adjusted gross income of the private sector	
		(Billions of current dollars)	(Billions of dollars at 1939 prices)
1929	122	90·4	74·1
1930	117	77·1	65·9
1931	105	62·3	59·3
1932	94	45·1	48·0
1933	90	42·2	46·9
1934	96	49·8	51·9
1935	98	56·5	57·5
1936	98	64·2	65·5
1937	103	71·1	69·0
1938	101	64·9	64·3
1939	100	68·8	68·8
1940	102	77·4	75·9
1941	110	98·6	89·6

Statistical appendix

Note 7. Adjusted profits before and after taxes in current and 1939 dollars for the period 1929–40 are given below. Adjusted profits before taxes in current dollars are obtained as the difference of the adjusted gross income of the private sector and adjusted private wages and salaries as given in Note 5. Adjusted profits after taxes are obtained by deducting *all* direct taxes both corporate and personal (direct taxes on workers having been small in the period considered). Finally, adjusted profits before and after taxes are deflated by the price index implicit in the deflation of the gross product of the private sector as given in Note 6.

| Year | Adjusted profits | | Adjusted profits | |
| | Before taxes | After taxes | Before taxes | After taxes |
	(Billions of current dollars)		(Billions of dollars at 1939 prices)	
1929	45·2	41·2	37·0	33·7
1930	36·7	33·4	31·4	28·5
1931	28·1	25·7	26·7	24·5
1932	19·0	17·2	30·2	18·3
1933	17·8	15·8	19·8	17·6
1934	21·9	19·6	22·8	20·4
1935	26·7	23·9	27·3	24·4
1936	29·9	26·2	30·5	26·8
1937	33·2	28·8	32·2	27·9
1938	30·4	26·5	30·1	26·2
1939	32·0	28·1	32·0	28·1
1940	37·1	31·6	36·3	31·0

Note 8. The sum of gross private investment, the export surplus, the budget deficit and brokerage fees is given on p. 190. This sum is equal to gross savings plus brokerage fees (see p. 91). The corresponding 'real' values are obtained by using as a deflator the index implicit in the deflation of the gross product of the private sector (see Note 6).

† Source of data used: U.S. Department of Commerce *National Income Supplement to Survey of Current Business*, 1951.

Note 9. Correlating the adjusted real profits after and before tax, P and π, as given in Note 7, we obtain the following regression equation:

$$P = 0.86\pi + 0.9$$

The correlation coefficient is equal to 0.991.

Year	Gross private investment plus export surplus plus budget deficit plus brokerage fees	
	(Billions of current dollars)	(Billions of dollars at 1939 prices)
1929	17.3	14.2
1930	11.9	10.2
1931	5.8	5.5
1932	3.0	3.2
1933	3.1	3.4
1934	5.8	6.0
1935	8.2	8.4
1936	11.4	11.6
1937	11.1	10.8
1938	9.1	9.0
1939	12.9	12.9
1940	16.2	15.9

C. NOTES TO CHAPTER 10

Note 10. The data on the volume of gross investment in fixed capital and the volume of the gross product of the private sector are given below. Fig. 10.2, which was used in the discussion of the 'acceleration principle', is based on these data.

Correlating gross investment with gross product and with time, t, we obtain the following regression equation:

$$\text{investment} = 0.306 \, (\text{product} - 1.45t) - 14.5$$

where t is counted in years from the beginning of 1935. In Fig. 10.2 there are shown the deviations of both sides of this equation from the mean. Thus fluctuations in gross investment in fixed capital and fluctuations in gross product are compared after they have been reduced to the same amplitude and the intervening trend has been eliminated.

Statistical appendix

Year	Gross investment in fixed capital	Gross product of the private sector
	(Billions of dollars at 1939 prices)	
1929	13·5	81·5
1930	10·2	73·5
1931	7·1	67·7
1932	4·0	57·4
1933	3·5	56·5
1934	4·4	62·0
1935	5·8	67·6
1936	7·9	76·4
1937	9·3	80·9
1938	7·2	76·4
1939	9·5	83·7
1940	11·4	92·1

INDEX

193

Index

consumption
  total + investment = national income, 1 n, 36, 39
  in business cycle, 27, 29, 96, 98, 135
  national, determination of, 93–104
  opposition to subsidies to, 140, 142, 143
  relation between investment and (Tugan-Baranovski), 147–8
consumption goods
  demand for, by workers in investment-goods industries, 12, 29, 31, 32
  ratio of prices of investment goods and of, 60–1, 124
  rise in prices with capacity production of, 81 n, 168–9
  production of, not aim of capitalism, 146
corporations, giant, 49–50, 51–2, 54, 55
cost-determined prices, 43–4
cost of living, 164
costs
  prime, difference between sales and = gross profit, 36
  taxation on wage-goods and, 37–8
  and prices, 43–61, 168
credit inflation, 13
currency, devaluation of, 22–3

demand, problem of effective, 146–55
demand-determined prices
  of raw materials, 43–4, 58, 64
  of finished goods at full utilisation of equipment, 81 n, 168–9
depreciation of capital equipment, 6, 114, 118, 119 n
  relation of investment to, in business cycle, 128, 129, 130, 131, 171 n, 179–81
depression, in business cycle, 11
  export surplus as way out of, 15
  unemployment in, 26, 31, 96, 137
  wages and prices in, 26–8, 69–73
  'protection' of profits in, 50–1, 57, 65, 70, 90–2
  salaries in, 73, 75
  investment in, 74, 98
  savings in, 131, 133
  'floor' of, 133

government intervention to alleviate, 138, 142–5
devaluation of currency, 22–3
'distribution factors', 80–1, 95
dividends
  'squeezing' of, 108
  ratio of, to share prices, 113
doles, effects of payment of, 18, 33
Douglas, Paul H., 53, 184

employment, full
  in socialist system, 97
  in business cycle, 130, 137, 169
  political aspects of, 138–45
  trade-union power and, 163
exports
  surplus of, 15–18, 23, 24–5
  'domestic', 18–24
  in theory of profits, 81–2, 83, 84–6, 90–2
  in determination of national income, 99
  as mainspring of capitalist growth (R. Luxemburg), 146, 151–5

fascism, and full employment, 141–2
finished goods, price-formation for, 43, 58–61
firms, size of, 105–9
foreign capital, influx of, 21–2, 25
foreign credits, 15
foreign currency
  influx of, 15 n, 19
  outflow of, 21, 22
foreign debts, 15
  servicing of, 21, 22
Fowler, B. M., 57

gold
  influx of, 15 n, 19, 85 n
  outflow of, 21, 22
government
  payments to employees of, 68 n, 94
  spending by: as 'domestic exports', 18–24; to maintain full employment, 138, 142–5; market created by, 147, 153–5
growth of capitalist economy, and business cycle, 165–83

Hilgerdt, F., 68
holding companies, 107

Index

Index